Crazy Dogs & Crazy People

LOOKING AT BEHAVIOR

IN OUR SOCIETY

by
Ernest Pecci, M.D.
and
C. W. Meisterfeld

M R K Publishing

The Publishing House Truly Dedicated to Man's Best Friend

Library of Congress Catalogue
No. 92081548

ISBN 0-9601292-7-8

M R K Publishing
448 Seavey
PETaluma, CA 94952

ACKNOWLEGMENTS

Computer Entry — Tammy, you were exceptionally patient in wading through all the handwritten material. Many thanks for your persistence.

A-to-Z Desktop — John and Meredith Schwirtz, your willingness (to serve) came to light after our third rewriting/editing and typesetting. Meredith, a great big hug for all the graphic redesigning.

The Editors — James Howland and Kristine Blakely. Many thanks for your sharp eyes and pencils.

The Illustrator — Walt Lee, what goes around comes around. Oceans do not separate friendships.

Backcover Illustrator — Illustration & Graphic Design: Kelly, you did an excellent work of art. Two heads are better than one.

Karl Ortiz, Ph.D., Anthropologist/Psychologist
Many thanks for contributing your anthropology references concerning how tribal communities were transformed from friendly to war-like and vice versa inside of a very short time period of one or two generations. *As their environment changed their behavior changed.* This confirms my statement how every important environmental conditioning is. E.P.

Winnie — Your faith and support through all my learning years will never be forgotten (1435 has been). C.W.M.

To my wife Noma, who patiently helped me to translate my technical writing into layman's language (you're the boss). E.P.

The Quaker Oats Company:
Thanks for your permission to publish your annual 'Dog Hero of the Year' stories. An extra special thanks to Cynthia Bauer (of M.P.F.C.) who took the time to locate the supportive photos.

WANTED: BRAVE AND HEROIC CANINES
If you know of a dog that has performed a heroic deed, write to Dog Hero of the Year, P.O. Box 1370, Barrington, IL 60011.

The Harvard Medical School Health Letter
Thank for granting us the right to reprint "Dog Bites and Children's Faces," *The Harvard Medical School Health Letter*, 11/1984.

FORWARD

This book offers, in an easy to read and anecdotal fashion, the combined half century experience of the authors in working with human and dog behavioral problems. Through their long-standing collaboration, which led to an understanding of the parallels between dog and human behavior, the authors have succeeded in greatly simplifying the complex variables involved in human and dog behavior and have clarified a number of misconceptions that have heretofore been widely accepted regarding the proper methods of training dogs and rearing children.

The book format is designed to alternate chapters by each author (designated by the letter "P" or "M") in a way which sometimes parallels the other and sometimes expands into new areas of their own expertise.

MRK Publishing

Dr. Ernest Pecci is a Board-certified Psychiatrist, practicing in the Bay Area for the past 25 years. He embodies the unique combination of a conservative Bostonian background and professional training with his active involvement as a pioneer in the New Age movement beginning in the early 1950's.

Following his honorable discharge from the Navy, Dr. Pecci returned to his education at Tuft's Medical School, in Boston. Upon graduation, he interned at Chelsea Naval Hospital and then moved to California for a residency in Psychiatry at Langley Porter Neuropsychiatric Institute in San Francisco.

In 1968, Dr. Pecci became the first Medical Director of the two innovative George Miller, Jr., Centers for Handicapped Children and Adults in Contra Costa County, a position he held for ten years.

In 1969, he founded, and is President Emeritus of, Rosebridge Graduate School of Integrative Psychology, in Concord, California, the only State-approved doctorate program in psychology in Contra Costa County.

Dr. Pecci's professional experience includes Chief Psychiatrist for the California Youth Authority in Sacramento (1980-1985). During this period, he was President of the Association for Past Life Research and Therapy and was largely responsible for this organization's current high level of professional membership.

C.W. Meisterfeld has 40+ years in the dog world. His philosophy of *Mutual Respect* and *Training Without Pain* has earned him the Canine Distinction Award for A.K.C. Obedience (1957) and National Retriever Championships for three consecutive years — 1962, 1963, and 1964 — with a perfect 500 score in 1962. He is the pioneer of canine psychoanalysis and psychological dog training (1963). Meisterfeld teaches canine behavioral psychology in California's colleges and universities. He is a member of the National Speakers Association and is considered the first canine psychoanalyst to be recognized/approved in the judicial system of the United States (California's Superior Court, 1982).

Contents

Color Photos/Graphs

INTRODUCTION
by Dr. Pecci

Much research has been done to examine the numerous variables which determine human behavior. I have found that the understanding of behavior can be immensely simplified by understanding a few basic principles governing the behavior of social animals, and especially the dog.

Dogs provide an ideal prototype for the study of behavior in humans because they, like humans, are genetically social animals. Equally important, they are unique in their willingness to seek a bond of servitude to humans as strongly as with members of their own species. This makes them analogous to young children, at least in all the essential ways we need to understand the effects of early environmental conditioning, and especially the influence of different styles of training and discipline upon behavior.

The word "discipline," has negative connotations to most people because, in their own childhood, it was often associated with suppression or control. Discipline, as used here, is not equated with punishment, coercion, or suppression. These are all measures resorted to by an autocratic authority figure when discipline has failed. These, too, ultimately fail in their goal. Although initially they may gain outward compliance, they promote resentment, rebellion, or passive-aggressive resistance through escapism or apathy. The proper exercise of discipline is essential for teaching a young child how to modulate his impulses and to meet challenges and expectations with greater and greater levels of mastery so as to develop a positive self-concept. Since most of the important communication between young children and parents is non-verbal (actions and tone of voice carry more impact than words), we can find a number of parallels between their behavioral responses and the behavior of puppy dogs to an authority figure. If this appears to be an over-simplification, then all the better. Too often, children are treated as if they are tiny adults. On the contrary, they are bewildered, confused, in awe of adults and totally unable to comprehend the motives of adults. They cannot reason like adults because their frontal lobes, the reasoning part of their brains, is incompletely developed until after five years of age. All they experience is the intense need to be loved and to be found acceptable by their god-like caretakers. Their hypnotic-like suggestibility and susceptibility to the emotions of their parents gives to the parents a level of power over them that is unequaled in any other human relationship. Most parents are unaware of their power and commonly misuse it by careless, critical, harsh, or impatient rough handling which creates deep emotional wounds to the psyche of the child.

The relationship of a child to his parents necessarily changes as he evolves through the various developmental stages from total dependence, to imitation and identification and, finally, to autonomy and independence. It is important for a parent to understand the nature of their power to mold the behavior and self-image of their child, and to understand when to make a shift in their mode of discipline and their relationship to the child as he matures. In contrast, the relationship of a dog to its owner remains relatively constant throughout its lifetime. Nevertheless, during my twenty-five years as a child psychiatrist, during which I consulted with countless parents, teachers, social workers, and juvenile authorities, I have arrived at this dramatic realization: the early training and discipline of a young child up to the age of approximately four to five years, must follow the same basic principles as used by experienced dog trainers who train with mutual respect. A full understanding of the implications of this statement can remove the mystique from child-rearing and bring clear answers to the often asked question: "What did I do wrong?"

Again, during his early years, the child's understanding of himself and of the world is very limited, and even his capacity to understand complex relationships does not come until much later.

The child cannot possibly understand adult motives or reasons for requiring certain behaviors. Neither can he be expected to understand the "why's" of his own emotions and behavior. It is a period when he needs help developing control over his feelings and impulses. His ability to postpone gratification is very limited and his tolerance for frustration is minimal. He is dependent upon you, in your manner of

14

seeing and responding to him for a sense of self. At every moment of your relating or not relating, you are telling him who he is.

During the period of early training, the child is disciplined to behave in accordance with the rules and limits which you have decided are important and which you have decided to establish within the given environment.

Discipline, to be effective must be established upon a basis of mutual respect and trust, and requires minimal or no physical enforcement. The average parents have no idea how much influence they really have over their children's behavior and how they, themselves, inadvertently condition their children into the patterns of rebellion and defiance of which they complain.

Early training practices establish the foundation for all future relationship and communication between parent and child, as well as a dog owner and his newly-purchased puppy.

Mankind's survival is dependent upon a redirection of the aggressive drive toward humanistic, heroic, and moral endeavors. These options must be taught by our educational system and by the television media. The innate desire to serve in a special way, to rescue an endangered loved one by an act of heroism, even the willingness to sacrifice one's life for a patriotic cause is much more a characteristic of the human spirit than the urge to seek recognition through an act of senseless violence. The key is the presence or the lack of a firmly established emotional bond. A devotional bond has motivated even dogs into countless acts of heroism which have been recorded over the centuries.

It is our aim as authors to 1) educate the public to becoming more aware of the responsibility we have in shaping the self-concept and the behavioral habits of our children, to 2) identify some of the destructive consequences of self-serving practices by people in authority on all levels which threaten the survival of our democratic society, and to 3) modify the unrealistic expectations for performance in our culture that are leading us further and further away from our essential nature as spiritual beings.

INTRODUCTION
by C.W. Meisterfeld

After centuries of devotion, servitude, and companionship to mankind our dogs are being sold down the river. They have become a throw-away object in our "instant" society. There are dog owners who lose interest in the cute, fluffy puppy once it grows up and becomes too big to live in the house. This once-loved puppy becomes an ignored and neglected animal that is chained to a tree in the backyard. Once the dog starts barking for the attention and affection he was used to receiving he becomes a nuisance and the neighbors file a complaint. The owners now have an excuse to dump off their once-loved dog at the animal shelter and after 3-5 days of boarding, the unwanted pet is destroyed.

Many owners don't even try to find out the cause or fix it. They simply replace their misbehaved dog with a new one. Others use the quick fix recommended by experts and beat their dog into submission or tranquilize him.

The message is reverberated to dog owners that increasing dog attacks have genetic reasons and are breed-specific. Presently, Pitbulls are considered the villains. One Humane Society in a large city killed thousands of dogs within a few weeks for the sole reason that they were either Pitbulls, American Stafford Terriers or had Pitbull characteristics. This slaughtering spree included any breed of dog with a pushed-in face, such as the Bulldog, the Pug and the Boston Terrier. All these dogs were considered *not adoptable* and received the death sentence.

How sad, how tragically sad! For all they have done for us, our dogs are rewarded with punishment and destruction!

The readers, especially those who are concerned about the welfare of our dogs, might be interested to learn how and when all this started.

The peaceful coexistence between man and dog became disturbed about twenty years ago, when a massive assault was launched in dog training based on a new theory called the "Alpha Dog." In its wake, the formerly amiable relationship deteriorated. The dog owning and training world was advised to mimic wolf behavior when interacting with dogs. This implied that the dog owner or trainer had to become the Alpha or top dog by physically dominating the pet. According to the recommendations, this position was to be established by picking up the puppy, scruff-shaking him, throwing him down, straddling him, and growling at him. Thus the dog was to be forced to submit to his human Alpha.

Ironically, brood bitches of domestic dogs neither have the habit of scruff-shaking their pups, nor of rolling them over, or pinning them down, when they misbehave, as every long-time breeder can confirm.

It is a shame that the dog world so readily accepted and followed this ridiculous and detrimental concept, which destroyed the respect of our dogs for mankind and for each other.

Before our dogs became the victims of this kind of abuse, adult dogs would not fight with a bitch or a puppy. Also, I have never known of a family dog that attacked a family member. When a young child got too rough or abusive, the dog would just get up and walk away without expressing any hostility.

When we observe the wolf's dominant behavior, we have to understand one basic law of nature. It is the law of survival, which rules the behavior of every creature. In this respect, the expression of dominance is very important in many wild-living animals for the continuance of the species through the survival of the fittest.

However, due to domestication and selective breeding, aggressive, dominant behavior not only completely lost its importance for the survival of our dogs, it even became a detriment.

Now, since forceful dominance has become an essential part of the interactions between owner and dog, our dogs are conditioned to accept and express this dominance as a principal behavior trait, like the wild-living animals. This hastens their demise in the human environment.

After specializing over a quarter of a century in dog behavior problems, my experienced conclusion is, that we are systematically destroying our dogs with these dominant concepts, no matter what breed. The authorities contribute their share by drafting vicious dog laws based on any breed that has caused a fatality. Even friendly breeds will be included. Some of the breeds whose aggressiveness was the reason for the cancellation of their owners' homeowners insurance, are the Chesapeake, German Shepherd, Akita, Chow, Collie, Dalmatian, Doberman, Husky, Malamute, Labrador Retriever, Newfoundland, Rottweiler, and various mixed breeds.

The only salvation for Man's Best Friend is to extinguish the darkness of ignorance and misinformation in his owner and to turn to the light of education.

CHAPTER 1(P)
TERRITORIAL BOUNDARIES AND LIMITS

From infancy, a child begins to learn about himself and about the material world through his play. It takes up to three years to comprehend fully the concepts of "in," and "out," "big," and "small," "up," and "down," and the permanence of material substances, even when they are out of sight. Gradually, through trial and error, he learns his limitations in regard to manipulating the material world. He also learns through parental admonition that there are things he can touch and things he must not touch, although the reasons are not always clear.

In a similar fashion the child gradually comes to terms with the real and dictated limits of his immediate environment. The healthy child is filled with the natural impulse to explore, examine, interact with, and to experience new frontiers in his world of wonderment. With each limit comes a sense of frustration. Not recognizing his mortality, he will exercise every sense organ and include fingers and mouth to explore the surfaces of every colorful object within his reach. Moving objects fascinate him, and he is even more delighted by his ability to move, spin, or pile them into configurations of his own choosing. This gives him his first sense of power. There is also the sensory component of his being which seeks constant stimulation. If, in his process of discovery, he takes a mild tumble, or rolls, spins, or swings after a momentary startle and a reassessment of his intactness, he will take delight in repeating the motor movements over and over again to keep his inner gyro spinning.

But, again, a limit is eventually set to the boundaries of his three dimensional world. A wise parent will child-proof an area of the house to minimize the repetitive "no" which abruptly puts a stop to the natural flow of the seeking of new experiences. A series of repeated "no's" at any age, can lead to a build up of frustration which can lead to a temper tantrum. A temper tantrum is the result of a child's loss of control over his frustration at being repeatedly blocked in the middle of an intended action.

21

Thus, early environmental conditioning is centered upon the core concept of setting limits. How this is done has a powerful impact upon both security and self-concept. It's as basic as "yes" and "no." An environment in which the "yes's" and the "no's" are predictable and consistent is a safe environment. When the "yes's" and "no's" are inconsistent and the no's harshly imposed, there is insecurity, resentment, and the urge to rebel.

As the child repeatedly tests the real and the arbitrary limits placed upon his movements, if these remain reasonably expansive and consistent, he will gradually accept and even experience a sense of safety within this finite area he now sees as "his ego space." Out of this a sense of territoriality arises. This is now his realm, and he may resent other children violating this space unless he can attain some type of dominance over them. Parents who inconsistently contract and expand the child's "world-space" foster a reaction of rebellion, defiance, or insecurity and fear.

In both dogs and children there comes a sense of security in knowing one's boundaries. In a real sense, it is having a predictable and safe space where freedom of movement is relatively unlimited, and there is a sense of personal possession attached to the objects within it. The lack of a well-defined boundary fosters a sense of being untethered or uncared for and, with this, a feeling of insecurity. It is not unusual for a child to provoke a spanking from a parent in order to elicit a sense of caring and to force an authority figure to define its behavioral boundaries. Children in therapy have commented to me: "My parents don't care what time I come home or where I go — they just don't care about me. John's parents spank him because they care."

The difference, here, between children and dogs is that a child's boundaries must gradually expand as he advances to the role of adult, while a dog's boundaries remain essentially constant. Setting clear and consistent emotional and physical limits is essential to maintaining a sense of security and to teach respect for the territorial space of others.

SETTING LIMITS

There is a right way and a wrong way to set limits. Limit-setting necessitates a prior decision on your part as to which behaviors will be tolerated and which will not be permitted. Then, there must be a consistent communication by both word and action of these limits before and during the times they are being tested by your dog, child, student, or whomever you have the responsibility to supervise, and it is a certainty that they will be tested. Keep in mind that the healthiest environment you can create is the one which imposes the fewest "no's" and "don't's." This includes keeping to a minimum the likelihood of the child being hurt, or articles being damaged, or that an embarrassing or upsetting mess can be made of the setting without your constant interference and control of the situation. In the case of a puppy dog or a young child, you must realize that they have only minimal control over their own behavior. The immediate environment may be too threatening, forbidden objects too seductive, and the restrictions too frustrating, or the expectations of "good" behavior too unrealistic. An understanding of the energy that is being expressed by a particular behavior, *i.e.*, curiosity, excitement, etc., is necessary to appropriately prevent or to terminate it. This means being alert to the buildup of tension so as to defuse or re-channel it while it is manageable. To interrupt the natural flow of any intent or expression in midstream is guaranteed to provoke inner rage.

You can easily understand that screaming at a child for behavior over which he has minimal control can be devastating to his self-image. And chastising a child for a behavior he learned indirectly through your modeling, or, to inconsistently expand and contract his limits is "crazy-making."

Thus, it is necessary that you, as an adult, must be responsible for, and in control of, your own behavior at all times. Otherwise, you will become emotionally reactive to unwanted behavior, giving up your power to the child and to consequently be reduced to coping with the situation at the child's level. Remember, the child is not capable of setting his own limits, and not being given limits can drastically reduce his sense of security.

There is an innate need in humans to have a safe haven, a home base, a place they can call their own to return to after traveling, exploring, or fighting a war. Thus, we have factions, cliques, fraternities, and countries fighting for their territorial boundaries.

Parents often do not realize how important a child's territorial space is to him and so inadvertently frequently violate it causing "unexplainable" fits of temper. For example, the introduction of a new baby into the home has to be done with a sense of understanding how this can provoke a high level of anxiety and resentment in the child. The same response of indignant resentment will be expressed by a dog when a new puppy is brought into the environment. And witness how differently children relate to a friend depending upon whether they are visiting his house or he is visiting theirs. There is a general pattern in both prepubescent boys and girls (ages 10-13) to be more passive, obliging, and willing to "fit in," when at the home of a playmate. Conversely, when they are the host/hostess in their own home they set the tone, direct the activities, and generally take on the airs of the "person in charge." I observed this in my own son, who was somewhat reticent and shy during his early teens in the company of his friends when in their homes, but would take on a noticeably dominant attitude when his friends came to visit to play computer games on his turf.

Even relatively restricting limits will be accepted as a safe or cozy home base without provoking resentment or resistance, depending upon how the limit was set. If it is not set with the energy of caring and respect, then it will be resented and rebelled against as does a prisoner to his prison cell. A common example of this occurs when parents place their child in a crib or in an enclosed outdoor area to get them out of the way, to be free from them. The child receives "don't exist" messages, which arouse his survival instincts and cause him to whimper or howl until he receives some kind of attention, even if it is negative attention, which is better than none.

If there is no respect for the limit-setter in the home, there will be no respect for limit-setting by the authorities that control the greater society. Without mutual respect and caring, constant force is needed to maintain territorial limits. We see this among neighboring countries everywhere in the world today.

An example of the result of disrespect for any outside authority to establish safe territorial boundaries, is the increasing tendency of youth to regress atavistically back to pack behavior, as seen in the street gangs of most major cities, where territorial boundaries are protected with whatever violence is necessary.

Civilization, by its definition, implies a structure with a socializing veneer which keeps violent tendencies in check. And this certainly appears to be true within the confines of a homogenous culture, especially when the man of each household has a significant place and role in the sustaining of that culture. In "polite society," the majority of the citizens willingly conform to the social pressures which temper aggression. However, as the social structure weakens, so too does its protective socializing restraint upon aggression and violence.

While we must be cautious as to the danger of directly comparing human behavior to animal behaviors, there are some suggestive examples that help give insight into our own innate propensities under particularly stressful environmental conditions. Dr. Frederick Goodwin, newly appointed Director of the National Institute of Mental Health, sees some noteworthy parallels between the violent behavior of young male rhesus monkeys and that of young, male human beings.

Goodwin suggests that the rise of inner-city violence might be the result of a loss of 'civilizing' social factors comparable to those in a monkey society that usually keep the adolescent male's naturally violent behavior in check. Studies show that when young males leave the restraining social fabric of a monkey troop, as they do at a key stage in their lives, some become hyperaggressive, and even murderous. Goodwin suggests that the loss of structure in human society might be similarly responsible for the upsurge in urban violence.

CHAPTER 2(M)
THE TERRITORIAL MIND

Dogs are very sensitive about territorial boundaries. Because they feel threatened, most dogs will react aggressively and bite when their territorial safety region is invaded. Their most critical zone, the personal safety range, where a dog feels he is within the reach of an adversary, is about 5 to 8 feet. Their general territorial zone is 15 to 20 feet. This is their flight distance. The more fearful a dog, the greater the flight distance he needs. At a certain point, he will retreat, at another he will attack when a person or animal he perceives as hostile is within his critical territory.

When a dog feels cornered and has no possible avenue to escape, he will become very frightened and act in self-defense on the spot, either by giving a warning signal with a growl, or by biting immediately without warning. Therefore, it is very dangerous to try to pet a strange dog in a car or a dog tied up or confined in a yard. Most dogs take their job of guarding their owner's property VERY seriously and express that by barking and/or biting when a stranger enters their territory.

While a dog is feeding he may respond aggressively as his owner approaches due to his territorial sensitivity. If the owner condones the dog's threatening attitude he actually strongly conditions this territorial demand of the dog. The owner should never accept this behavior from his dog, but instead he should attempt to desensitize his pet. Some dogs extend their safety zone over the critical distance of about 15 to 20 feet no matter where they are. Stepping into a dog's safety range always involves risks.

Our domestic dogs have a psychological need for their owners to define the territorial boundaries for them. This includes physical (house, yard) and psychological (in a behavioral sense) boundaries. This need separates man's best friend from the rest of the animal kingdom, including the wolf. It is of paramount importance that training to establish the territorial limits take place as soon as the puppy comes into your home and before it is four to five months old, thus preventing a lot of behavior problems. As a dog develops his learning ability, he self-teaches based on his daily experiences of self-gratification and adrenal stimulation. If uncontrolled, his territorial boundaries constantly expand. First, his home/yard is his domain to be protected. Then the next door neighbor's yard, followed by one or several city blocks, is annexed into his territory. In his kingdom, he will challenge any intruder, be it four-legged or human.

TERRITORIAL BOUNDARIES

Dogs' territorial behavior is mainly based on survival instincts and protective feelings of guarding his owner's properties. It is one of the things I watch for when a dog comes to me for testing with a background of territorial aggressiveness, biting/attacking any intruder who enters his/her territory. A dog with a well-balanced nature has an inner and exact instinct and knowledge of his boundaries, such as the small Chihuahua owned by a neighboring rancher. When he sees me doing my brisk walk past his owner's house he will start barking about 60 feet away from me, trotting down the driveway right up to the edge of the driveway and road, stopping on his invisible territorial boundary line, still barking.

But, when I meet his mistress out on the road and away from her property, the dog does not start barking at me when he spots me coming from the opposite direction, greeting each other as we pass by on our separate walks. The tiny dog expresses a friendly, non-protective behavior and even runs up to me wiggling and wanting to be petted. Although this friendly meeting on neutral ground has been going on for several years, he still becomes protective on his own property when the owners are not present.

This is instinct and it can and should be reinforced with psychological training. A well-balanced dog expresses this natural behavior of knowing his home territorial boundaries from the strange ones outside his lines.

This is very important when I need to test a dog who has a case history of attacking/biting. His ability to shrink his territorial protecting behavior when his owner takes him out of the car into my parking lot is the first evaluation. The next one is as the owner walks through the office/kennel doorway. I watch the dog's body language. Does he walk in with the attitude of King Kong, "This is my turf," with his tail up and stiff and very positive/assertive walking movements, or does he hesitate and pause using the element of time for discrimination — a cautious Jack. Body language is their main mode of expressing behavior. If the dog expresses the "King Kong" attitude, this tells me that his natural territorial respect is not in operation.

TERRITORIAL PROTECTIVENESS

A serious problem in connection with a dog's territorial protectiveness is that mail carriers employed by the U.S. Postal Service, United Parcel, and Federal Express, as well as other service personnel such as meter readers, etc., are experiencing an increasing number of dog attacks and bites. A young lady who very much enjoyed her job as a mail carrier and had loved dogs all her life told me what she had experienced recently:

"I was inserting mail in a family's mailbox where I had delivered mail for quite some time without problems, when I was suddenly attacked by a dog who came from behind the house. Even though I managed to prevent being bitten by slowly backing out of the yard, this negative experience left a deep scar in my mind. Although the postal service issued a warning to the dog's owner after this incident, saying the mail delivery would be subject to confinement of the dog, I turned in my resignation within two weeks. They offered me an inside position in which I was not interested. I had taken the carrier job for the outdoor experience and the walking exercise which now I was unable to continue due to my fear. My problem is that I cannot help but recall this ferocious dog flying at me with all four feet off the ground. It is like a recurring nightmare. I become almost paranoid when I encounter a dog, and so does my eight-year-old son, whom I unfortunately infected with my fear."

29

SUMMARY

1. Most dogs are territorial and protective when on their own property.

2. The most critical territorial range for a dog, his personal safety zone, is within five to eight feet.

3. When a dog feels cornered with no avenue to escape and becomes fearful, he will bite . . . even his owner.

4. Every dog has the psychological need for his owner to define his territorial and behavioral limits, and to condition him through training.

5. Without training, the dog's physical and behavioral boundaries will constantly expand until there are no more limits.

6. When you permit your dog to define his own boundary lines, he can become a hazard to service personnel who need to enter your property.

7. Being surprised by such an overly protective dog can be a traumatic experience for life. The affected service person can transmit this phobia to other family members, including children.

CHAPTER 3(P)

AGGRESSIVE BEHAVIOR AND VIOLENCE

Violence and the fear of violence has become a major concern of every citizen of this country today. Supposedly, the most technologically advanced and humane culture on the planet, few of our public parks and streets are safe at night. As the statistics for rape and murder spiral upward yearly, significantly so do the incidents of vicious attacks within the family by the family dog, which was almost unheard of in the past.

Are we creating the potential for violence within our young or has our civilization become too complex to put constraints upon the natural propensity for violence that was always there?

Everyday we read in the newspapers new appeals to curb violence by winning the war against drugs, by establishing gun control laws, and by building more prisons and putting tougher penalties on criminals. None of the above, even if carried out to a high degree of success, will have any significant effect upon reducing violence. We hear that poverty, prejudice, stress, and job frustration all contribute to violence. But this is only partly true. Otherwise, why was violence such a rare event during the Great Depression of the 1930's when I was growing up?

I remember when I was ten years old how a senseless rape and murder in the Boston suburb where I was raised created a wave of shock that lasted for many weeks even after the young man was apprehended. Today, and especially in the major cities, incidents of rape and murder have become so commonplace that they barely make the news-of-the-day on the front page.

Interestingly, dog viciousness against children has been getting increasing attention. We can learn a lot from this because viciousness in dogs and violence in humans have common roots. Guns, drugs, and poverty have little to do with it. Surely, defanging a dog will reduce his potency, but will not cure the problem. The problem lies in the fact that we are breeding violence in our children and our young adults faster than we can control it by counter-punitive means.

During my years of working as a psychiatrist in the California Youth Authority, I became intrigued with the issue of violence. I saw hundreds of teenagers incarcerated for senseless crimes. Drugs and weapons were often involved, and most came from poor neighborhoods. Yet, how many people in this country have taken drugs and not felt the urge for violence? How many people have access to guns or knives without the compulsion to use them? I, myself, was raised in poverty all through the depression, and the thought of a violent act of any kind never came into my head.

One of the reasons there is so much controversy around the causes and the control of violence is that there is a tendency to link anger, frustration, and violence together in one package, whereas they are only indirectly linked. *Violence is a learned or environmentally conditioned behavior that can be extinguished through proper rearing experiences in both children and pets.*

Before I review the thinking process by which I and other researchers in the field are arriving at this conclusion, I want to point out that this is strongly validated by anthropologists who have noted that an isolated island population of totally passive and peaceful tribal people can be transformed into a warlike, violent population within two generations.

At this point, let us propose a basic definition of violence: *"Violence is premeditated, excessive use of force directed toward a target victim with the intent to inflict pain and suffering."* "Intent" is the key word here. Is the intent survival, *i.e.*, self-protection, is the intent to obtain food, is it for sport, or is it to obtain revenge for a past act of aggression?

The motives for violence may be complex and the emotions which accompany it such as anger, fear, frustration, etc., vary widely. More often we are shocked at the "cold-blooded" nature of violence in which relatively little guilt or remorse is experienced afterwards. Courts of law seek mitigating circumstances such as drugs, "uncontrollable impulse," provocation, self-defense, and "temporary insanity" to forgive acts of violence. However, we know that schizophrenics and those labelled legally insane are no more prone to violence than the general population. Diabetics and people suffering from hypoglycemia (albeit the famous Twinky case, where Dan White was given a light sentence for murdering the mayor and a supervisor because he ate a pastry beforehand) do not become violent. The average person who imbibes alcohol or who takes LSD does not act violently. Generally, the perpetrator of violence feels little or no remorse for his actions since it is the result of a learned behavior that he inwardly is convinced was justifiable under the circumstances. On the contrary, perpetrators of violence are more likely to become exhilarated at the retelling of their perpetrations and, at best, feign remorse when confronted with the suffering of their victims.

Dozens of young men whom I interviewed, who had committed senseless violence, and most of whom were otherwise friendly and likable in a prison setting, all describe in different terms their experience of excitement and exhilaration (the adrenal rush described in greater detail later), and the sense of personal power accompanied by a gratifying release of pent-up rage, hurt, and frustration which brings with it a lingering "high" that can be addictive, like cocaine. It must be clearly stated: *violent behavior is highly addictive in both humans and animals.* This helps to explain why the greatest predictor of violent behavior is a previous history of violence. This principle also applies to violence against one's own body. Even relatively minimal acts of violence against the self, such as wrist cutting in a suicidal gesture can bring an experience of stimulation coupled with a release of emotional pain so that self-mutilization might thereafter become an impulse tendency. There is a large population of otherwise non-violent self-mutilators in the general population, who often call themselves, "cutters," most of whom were emotionally or sexually abused as children. The relief they experience from the cutting and the bleeding provides an example of how some people receive pleasure from pain. This includes pain inflicted upon themselves or pain inflicted upon a victim. I interviewed a youthful murderer once, who confided that cutting his victim's throat was a way of releasing the tension in his own throat.

There is no denying the powerful imprinting which being the object of violence or sexual abuse has upon a young child. The majority of child molesters were, themselves, molested as children. One young man I interviewed, told me that when he was six years of age he was kidnapped and sexually molested by an 18-year-old boy. When he himself reached the age of 18 years, he felt compelled to molest a six-year-old boy, the crime for which he had been incarcerated.

Anger, hostility, and aggression are not synonymous with violence. Some aggression is healthy and, perhaps, necessary as a motivating factor when properly channeled to accept challenges and to gain mastery through difficult accomplishments.

Some anger, in the course of everyday frustrations is unavoidable, but rarely leads to violence. When it is forcibly suppressed, or for other reasons insufficiently expressed, it may fester within and create a cumulative effect with time. But even this is more likely to result in psychosomatic illnesses (headache, ulcers, heart problems) than in violent behavior, in the average person. Most people occasionally experience a fleeting flush of anger which might result in throwing something across the room, kicking a chair, or screaming obscenities, but not, except in fantasy, result in a direct act of violence against a person. In fact, many therapy groups encourage the verbal release of pent-up anger as a way of releasing tension and reaffirming self esteem.

Negative, hostile, and violent feelings almost always emerge in the treatment of adolescents, and often they represent a way of relating and indicate that a bond exists. The expression of hostility is not curative nor an end in itself, yet part of the process of acceptance and mastery of feelings. It is an important learning process to the alternative of violent behavior.

THE BIOLOGICAL ROOTS OF ANGER

Anger springs from the deepest and most primitive part of the brain. Electrodes placed against the hypothalamus of cats can induce instant rage at the flip of a switch. The cerebral cortex, the reasoning part of the brain, covers and controls these inner primitive centers. Walter Cannon, the famous physiologist from Harvard University, was intrigued by his discovery in the 1930's that the removal of the cerebral hemispheres resulted in an extraordinary exhibition of rage. Similarly, anything that disturbs the regulatory function of the cerebral cortex, *i.e.*, brain damage, drugs, alcohol, malnutrition, and chronic stress, can result in increased irritability, intolerance to stress, frustration, and acts of violence.

Anger blocks thinking and creativity, constricts the flow of blood to the internal organs, holds the heart in a tight grip and, literally, blinds us to the potential for loving communication with others. When a person is in a state of extreme rage, his body is flushed with adrenalin and the rational part of the brain is partially paralyzed. All behavior is momentarily under the control of instinctive survival reactions or learned responses from earlier experiences and the modeling examples of adults who experienced rage during childhood.

Rage reactions such as temper tantrums, throwing the hammer you accidentally hit your finger with, screaming, loud complaining over a traffic citation, and threats against the dog next door for knocking down your garbage cans cannot be included in the category of violence. These represent episodes of momentary partial loss of emotional control.

One of the most uncomfortable revelations patients discover, during the course of personal analysis, is the volcano of inner rage that had been covered over with polite behavior (see *Illustration*, p. 136).

Where does all this anger come from? Karl Menninger believed that the human infant begins his life in anger. Even the most attentive mother may arouse a rage reaction in her baby when she doesn't respond immediately to his cries of hunger. Later, he may hate the newborn baby sister for diverting mother's attention from him.

However, unless anger is sanctioned in the environment, it quickly goes underground in order to buy love.

Fritz Redl, author of the book, *Children Who Hate*, claims that the hate mass is formed during the baby's first two years, and that its size depends upon the amount of genuine affection the baby receives and how much independence he is permitted. Emotional impoverishment results in a flood of fury at the slightest frustration, which a healthy child might quickly check by shifting toward an enjoyable substitute activity. However, children who have no happy memories to fall back upon will seek a target to attack to modulate their tension. But even here, the expression of anger will be based upon what they learned directly or indirectly from their parents in their own handling of anger.

All behavior results from attitude. Anger always justifies itself. Reality becomes distorted as emotion skews perceptions. Arguments only add fuel to the fire, both parties saying to themselves: "Again, I'm not understood." "Again, I'm always the one who's wrong." "Again, no one cares how I feel."

Because of our ingrained patterns of response, and the power of the emotions associated with these, we can, at best, have only limited and temporary control over our behavior unless we change the underlying attitude which prompts the behavioral responses. These attitudes, regarding ourselves and the world we live in, come both from our parents and from our educational system.

Anger is always a call for help, an expression of a defeat, of not being able to use more creative ways to maintain one's integrity. An example might be seen in children teasing each other. The one who fails to come up with a clever retort becomes enraged. Hate, regardless of how it is demonstrated, is usually the outgrowth of self-hate, and the less emotionally mature the individual, the more he hates, and the more he will obsess about sadistic fantasies for revenge. While such an individual may never actually become violent, he will inevitably become self-destructive in his close relationships.

The discussion of violent behavior would be incomplete without addressing the issue of temperament. There are a growing number of psychiatrists who believe that there is a biochemical or genetic predisposition to violent behavior. There is no denying the link of testosterone to aggressive behavior. Boys are significantly more aggressive than girls in their play. Males are responsible for up to 90% of all violent crimes. More recently, a number of studies have indicated an abnormally low level of serotonin in the blood of men predisposed to criminality. Serotonin is a hormone implicated in affective or mood disorders. The amino acid, tryptophan, is a precursor of serotonin and is found in most foods. Some recent studies have shown a lowering of blood serotonin in people who are dieting on low cholesterol diets and that this increases their level of chronic irritability and hostility. Chromosome abnormalities have also recently been detected in individuals predisposed to criminality.

All humans, and animals to a lesser degree, exhibit individual differences from birth in their reactivity to the environment. At least a dozen different personality characteristics can be readily observed in new-borns in the nursery, including sensitivity, the need for cuddling, irritability, crying, general motor activity, etc. Behavior, in all living organisms, is the outcome of the environment acting upon genetic potential. Out of this fact has come the nature-versus-nurture debate as to which has predominant importance. The higher the organism is upon the evolutionary chain, measured by the development of the brain and the neurological system, the more significant are the environmental factors which shape behavior.

I have found that a good environment can modify or override the behavioral problems of many hyperaggressive children. This also appears to be borne out in research with rhesus monkeys.

Steven Suomi, head of research of a rhesus monkey colony run by the National Institute of Child Health and Development, reported that the most aggressive monkeys had the lowest level of blood serotonin, genetically. However, what mattered most in determining personality was the environment and the kind of mothering the monkey received. Young monkeys, born with low serotonin, put into peer groups with an artificial mother that only supplied milk, were most likely to display violent behavior as adult monkeys. However, those placed with nurturing mothers grew up to be more normal.

Harry Harlow, experimenting on caged rhesus monkeys in the 1960's at the University of Wisconsin, showed that babies deprived of a mother grew up to be severely warped in personality, unable to fit into monkey society, and were prone to random acts of violence. However, he also showed that deprived and behaviorally impaired monkeys could be rescued by exposing them to younger, normal monkeys for as little as an hour a day. The same approach has been successfully applied in treating emotionally withdrawn human children.

CHAPTER 4(M)

UNPROVOKED ATTACKS AND FATALITIES

Presently, no one seems to be able to explain why a pet that has lived with a human family for years suddenly turns on a member of this very family, especially on little children.

I would like to share my non-clinical opinion regarding this phenomenon and an explanation based on my experiences and observations. Also, I want to focus attention on this subject to inspire more study and research.

One idea is that the main reason for the increasing vicious dog attacks is too much inbreeding, which weakens the genetic temperament of our dogs. Another hypothesis is that popular breeds are just bred for conformation of looks, and thus, the intelligence is bred out of the dogs. Another explanation is that the A.K.C. registered, purebreed dogs are not required to pass the working standards of their breed, such as herding dogs competing in herding trials, and hunting dogs required to pass field trial tests.

I agree with all these theories. However, they don't provide the complete answer to the problems. How can the occurrence of the same viciousness and dog fatalities caused by mixed breeds be explained? Many of the mutts involved were the result of accidental cross-breeding. Often it is not even possible to trace their heritage blood line.

In the late 1970's German Shepherds were considered the dangerous breed in the U.S. with a high occurrence of biting. That is a drastic change from what genetic experiments discovered at a Swiss psychological dog testing center called Fortunate Fields where German Shepherd police dogs were psychologically tested in 1934. Contrary to the prevailing opinion, to teach the German Shepherd to bite a man was the most difficult part of the police course. Certain, otherwise excellent, instructors were unable to make these dogs attack. No amount of teasing seemed to be able to overcome the dog's prejudice against violating the person of man. Of the 67 dogs (out of 100) that failed in the police course because of the "unwillingness to bite at any cost," 62 of them earned "average" to "excellent" for their friendliness and gentleness with children. Today, Pit Bulls are the main culprit. Other breeds, such as Rottweillers, Great Danes, and even Labradors are also involved in fatal biting.

THE HARVARD MEDICAL SCHOOL'S FINDINGS
DOG BITES AND CHILDREN'S FACES
(From the Harvard Medical Health Letter)

A relatively serious and unsolved public health problem is the high frequency with which dogs bite the faces of people, especially children. If results from a careful study conducted in Wisconsin hold true for the United States as a whole, there are some 44,000 facial injuries a year from dog bites, and of these 16,000 are severe. Almost all of the worst, and potentially disfiguring, injuries affect children under the age of 10. Treatment is made especially difficult by the fact that dog bites tend to tear delicate facial structures, such as eyelids and lips.

Although very little is known about the circumstances that lead to biting, some educated guesses can be made. Most bites appear to be inflicted by pets in familiar surroundings, and fewer than 6% are brought on by teasing or abuse. Many dogs normally bite each other around the head and mouth as part of aggressive play, and it may be that such dogs approach children in the same spirit, not reacting defensively and not "intending" to injure their victims. An innocent gesture of the child's may simply be misinterpreted by the dog as an invitation to bite.

The most obvious protective measures, reminding children to keep their faces away from dogs and keeping close watch on toddlers, are probably also the least effective, as Trudy Karlson, author of the Wisconsin study, observes. More stringent leash laws are also generally beside the point, as half of all facial bites to children under 4 are inflicted by their own pets, and 90% of the children in this age group are bitten while at home.

40

Probably the most useful step would be for families with young children to avoid keeping large, aggressive dogs as household pets. Unfortunately, little is known as to which breeds are apt to engage in facial biting. Some evidence indicates that working and sporting breeds pose the greatest risk, as do young dogs (males more than females). German Shepherds, Malamutes, and Huskies seem to be high-risk breeds, whereas hounds may have less inclination to bite than other breeds. Regardless of breed, dogs should never be left alone with a small child, even when the child seems to be protected by a playpen or crib. (*Journal of the American Medical Association.*)

THE U.S. HUMANE SOCIETY'S STATISTICS

Dogs' unique respect of mankind and refusal to bite does not appear to be the rule any longer according to the Humane Society's *Facts About Dog Bites*, prepared by Guy R. Hodge and Randall Lockwood.

"Dog bites are a serious medical problem. Each year in the United States, between 1 and 3 million dog bites are reported to public health agencies. It is estimated that between two to *forty* times that number of bites may go unreported! These unreported incidents usually involve less serious bites inflicted by a pet owned by the victim or victim's family. In general, we can conservatively estimate that in a typical year at least one in every 50 Americans is bitten by a dog.

"The majority of attacks take place on or near the dog owner's property. In most cases there has been no interaction between dog and victim immediately prior to the attack. Only 6% of the bites in one study were preceded by deliberate or accidental provocation. Bite incidents are often triggered by running or other rapid movement by the victim, which elicits a predatory chase response from the dog."

The following fatalities were compiled by the U.S. Humane Society in Washington D.C. and are not meant to create a paranoia of certain breeds. The intent is only to inform and alert the reader to the fact that all dogs have the propensity to attack and bite even when unprovoked. Their preferred victims are family members, especially chidren.

In ninety percent of the case histories of deaths due to dog bites, it was stated, "No prior history of aggression to the victim or toward anyone else." The few dogs that displayed prior aggressiveness were trained for protective or guarding purposes.

Inside of one year, the number of fatalities doubled from 12 in 1989 to 25 in 1990. Even more shocking is that the ages of the youngest child killed went from 2 years of age in 1989 to 5-day-old babies in 1990.

1989 FATALITIES

VICTIM	AGE	DOG BREED	LOCATION
Boy	2 years	One Pitbull	Garberville, CA
Boy	3 Years	Two Shepherd Crosses	Burlington, NC
Girl	3 years	One Wolf-Hybrid	Big Lake, MN
Boy	3 years	One Pitbull	Clute, TX
Girl	5 years	One Shepherd Cross One Malamute Cross	National Mine, MI
Man	20 years	Two Rottweilers	Winston-Salem, NC
Man	69 years	Bunch of Doberman Crosses	Dulzura, CA
Woman	72 years	Three English Bulldogs	Jacksonville, FL
Woman	72 years	One Terrier (Small)	Lyndonville, NY
Man	73 years	One Chesapeake Bay Retriever	Georgetown, DE
Woman	81 years	Two Dobermans	Bullhead City, AZ
Man	84 years	One German shepherd	Glouchester Cty, VA

1990 FATALITIES

VICTIM	AGE	DOG BREED	LOCATION
Girl	5 days	Husky	Florence, NJ
Boy	6 days	Husky	Lacey, WA
Girl	14 days	German Shepherd	Fort Meyers, FL
Boy	28 days	Wolf-Hybrid	Mat-Su Valley, AK
Boy	1 month	Chow	Ellabell, GA
Girl	1 month	Malamute	Pima County, AZ
Girl	2 months	Pitbull/Shepherd	Dalton, IL
Girl	6 months	Pitbull	Morgan Park, IL
Boy	18 months	Akita	Bremerton, WA
Girl	18 months	Pitbull	Melissa, TX
Girl	2.5 years	Wolf-Hybrid	Forest Township, MI
Boy	3 years	Husky/Malamute	Talkeetna, AK
Boy	4 years	Malamute	South Byers, CO
Girl	4 years	2 Mixed Breed Dogs	Coosada, AL
Boy	5 years	Rottweiler/Pitbull	Seneca, SC
Boy	10 years	Doberman	Odessa, TX
Woman	35 years	German Shepherd	West Palm Beach, FL
Woman	48 years	7 Mixed Breed Dogs	Walterboro, SC
Woman	57 years	2 Pitbulls	Memphis, TN
Woman	70 years	2 Pitbulls	Los Angeles, CA
Woman	72 years	Chow	Bryan, TX
Woman	72 years	Pitbull	West Memphis, TN
Man	81 years	Pitbull	Gwinette County, GA

DEATHS OF COMPANION ANIMALS

Our pets are also experiencing a drastic increase in the number of deaths. Approximately 18 million animals were killed in shelters in 1989. According to the **American Humane Society,** in 1990, 21.6 million joined them. That means that $2 billion of the taxpayers money was used to euthanize unwanted cats and dogs. According to

Susan Kane, the founder of *HART* and the editor of *MUTTMATCHERS MESSENGER*, despite these mind-boggling statistics, few shelters spay or neuter animals before allowing them to be adopted. This simple act alone would save millions of dollars.

DOG AGGRESSION INCREASE

I believe the root of increasing dog aggressiveness began around 40 years ago when dogs became possessions and symbols. I remember in the 1940's a lot of Ohio pheasant hunters used the Irish Setters because they had the natural retrieving instinct and did not range (hunt) beyond 40-50 yards, which was maximum distance for shooting with a shotgun. My own personal Irish Setter, Mabel, had all of these natural hunting instincts and required very little training.

In the early 1960's, a good Irish Setter was an exception rather than the rule. Today, this instinctual behavior that was once so dependable in a purebred hunting dog (and other breeds), does not seem to exist. This includes not only the breed's noted behavior, but also, the respect toward all smaller and weaker beings. It appears to me that when a dog owner does not take the necessary time to properly train a dog's mind based on mutual respect, the dog can only operate on his lower level of alpha/dominant or pecking order. This ancient aggressive behavior lies dormant in the depths of the dog's neurological pathways.

Also, when a dog does not receive any psychological training (based on respect), his innate instinct of willingness to serve, work, and respect the human family atrophies. This void in behavior is replaced by the ancient, self-directed, self-gratification and survival behavior of a wild animal. This is only speculative, but a thought worth considering.

CHAPTER 5(P)

BONDING AND ROLE CONFUSION

Most of my professional life has been devoted to teaching parents, teachers, and correctional officers how to discipline the infant child, the adolescent, or the young adult under their tutelage and care. My major task is always directly related to the problem of the unawareness and insensitivity of the person in authority as to the effects their own behavior has upon the mental state of their charge. I have found that making analogies to dog training can be very useful in bringing objective understanding to the true nature of the relationship.

For example, parents will complain that despite the fact that they are very firm, clear and directive with their young son, he still pouts or stubbornly resists obeying their wishes. I have them describe a specific incident and then ask: Suppose that you were invited to the home of a professional dog trainer who owned a pet German Shepherd. During the course of the evening, you hear the dog barking at a cat in the backyard which disturbs your conversation. Your friend shouts, "Rex." No response. With an angrier tone, he yells, "Rex," again. Finally, he gets up and drags the dog by the collar into the room, pushes him down beside his chair and gives his rump a sharp whack. The dog lets out a "yipe" and then remains frozen in his position. Would you be impressed with this performance? Definitely not, if you had ever witnessed the interaction between a properly disciplined German Shepherd and his master. You would never see a need for reprimand nor slapping.

Yet, in a similar situation, if the young son were playing too noisily in the other room, and he ignored a shout to "quiet down," you might be impressed with the parent who bodily yanks the child into the room, pats his fanny and firmly sits him down on a chair, where he remains quietly. I ask: What do you think is going on in the head of that child? And what kind of relationship is being established between the father and the child? Everything evolves around relationship.

This example is given because it appears to be a mild, "so-what" situation. But the child most likely experiences humiliation and deep-seated resentment because of a lack of sensitivity and respect for the special bond he thinks he had with his father. Would a respected adult friend be treated this way? In every encounter, always consider the effect of your behavior upon the long-term nature of the relationship. All future interaction is predicated upon this.

The need to bond with a strong, stable authority figure begins with the family unit. Because human behavior is more dependent upon learning than the behavior of lower animals, socialization of the child is primarily effected by identification with his parents, and the development of conscience reflects the parents' conscience, as well. Trust and respect for authority figures also begins in the home, first from the child's attitude toward the parents and secondarily, from the parents' attitudes toward teachers, religious leaders, and political figures in the greater community. The more consistent and warm the parents are toward the child, and the less authoritative or over-indulgent they are, the better the child's relationships with his peers.

Little boys and girls who try to help their fathers and mothers with household chores or gardening are devastated when they are criticized for "doing it wrong," or, "being clumsy," instead of being praised for their desire to form a loving partnership.

Arguments between the parents, provided there is some caring and an eventual resolution, can be a valuable learning experience for the child. However, altercations in which one parent belittles or verbally or physically abuses the other, creates considerable inner conflict inasmuch as the child identifies with both parents. Also, it is difficult for a child to receive love from a degraded parent without hating the other parent. A single-parent family in this case is far preferable, especially if there are visitation rights which allow the child to establish an independent bond with each parent.

A distinct generation boundary between a parent and child is essential to maintaining a mutual bond of respect and trust. However, sometimes, one parent will turn to the child for support against the other parent, or for reassurance, or to fill an emotional need. An extreme example of this is sexual molestation, which has devastating emotional consequences for the child.

A relatively more common breach of the "generation boundary" rule occurs when a guilty or needy parent with low self-esteem tries to buy love from a child by assuming a submissive, servitude pattern with constant catering to the child's every whim, thus forcing a dominance pattern upon the child. The child may become "spoiled," demanding, or confused regarding what to feel toward the parent. Behind this is a feeling of being manipulated or controlled. This servitude pattern in a mother can have an emotionally crippling effect upon a child. The child may grow into an emotionally immature and self-centered adult, dependent upon the mother and tending to marry late in life, if at all. Or the child, in a desperate attempt to gain autonomy, may try to maintain as much distance from mother as possible, while dutifully keeping a mechanical and polite relationship by telephone, preferably long-distance.

The need to gain acceptance and love by giving acceptance and love makes women, as a group, especially vulnerable to enabling behavior or co-dependent behavior. Men find a sense of significance through doing, impressing, and being a hero. Women find a sense of significance in giving nurturance and in giving of themselves freely to a man who resonates emotional pain similar to their own, and who appears to be starving for affection and love. However, in enabling a needy man, she perpetuates his sense of helplessness and immaturity and, eventually, he will become abusive in order to regain his autonomy and re-establish the masculine-dominant role. *This is a common syndrome experienced by women who "love too much."*

CHAPTER 6(M)

BONDING AND ROLE CONFUSION

Sue was very happy with her Great Dane puppy, Ronny, and the love and affection he expressed for her. She cuddled, stroked, and hugged him a lot, following the information she had read about the importance of bonding with the puppy at an early age, and that it can be intensified with lots of physical contact, such as hugging, kissing, picking the dog up and carrying him around. Sue, a true believer, followed this advice with Ronny as often as she could. Sue told me Ronny would lie on the couch with his head in her lap watching TV with her for hours. It seemed that the dog actually did view the programs. Ronny kept her feet warm by sleeping at the foot of the bed. (This was one of the reasons Sue had acquired a shorthaired dog.) Ronny loved to jog with Sue, and this was very easy for him, with his long legs. Ronny was very friendly to everybody, even to Sue's male clients and occasional weekend guests.

Sue's happiness was complete. She had a faithful companion who thrived on affection and returned it, who enjoyed the same things in life as she did, like TV soap operas and jogging. Plus he did not mind if she worked long hours in her business, which she operated out of her home. There was no need to negotiate "What should we have for dinner today?" or "Let's watch a different program!" There was never any reason for controversy, as it used to be with her ex-husband all the time. Sue was convinced her pet was the best deal she had ever made. A dream had come true, she had found the ideal partner for life.

If Sue had to leave the house and could not possibly take Ronny with her, a dog sitter would come over to keep the pet from getting lonely and bored. Sue could not live with the guilty feeling of forcing Ronny to go on a howling, moaning spree like "The Hound of the Baskervilles."

One time Sue had to be away from home for a couple of hours and could not take Ronny with her. Unfortunately, the sitter was not available and her neighbor did not have the spare time to keep Ronny company. Sue turned on the radio to drown out Ronny's howling blues, and hurried to finish her business. When she returned home, Ronny had expressed and manifested his "I missed you terribly." Not only had he been moaning the blues and chewing up Sue's bedspread, he also had had a spell of diarrhea in the bedroom. Sue never repeated this mistake. From then on she was faithful to Ronny. For the next two years they were always together, an inseparable pair.

One day Sue forgot her briefcase in her car. Ronny was sound asleep. So Sue quietly stepped out of the apartment door and rushed to the carport. The moment she reached her car, there was a loud smashing sound of breaking glass. Sue turned around abruptly, just in time to witness Ronny flying through her second-story bedroom window in a desperate attempt to remain at her side.

Miraculously, Ronny survived. No fractured bones, with only minor cuts from the broken window glass. The veterinarian who sutured the wounds suggested that Sue should seek some advice, and that there was a flaw in their relationship. Ronny was, without a doubt, humanized.

Usually, loving and affectionate dog owners expect the same in return from their pet. They are very disappointed when they don't get it and when the dog becomes demanding and reacts with jealousy, possessiveness, destructiveness, and other adverse behaviors, often culminating in biting instead of afffection. The problem is, we forget that a dog is a dog and not a human being who has different perceptions and means of self-expression. When a dog feels in danger (real danger or just an unknown situation he cannot cope with), he will bite as a natural reaction of self-defense.

By using his dog as a human substitute, object of worship and emotional satisfaction, the well-meaning dog owner overwhelms and frustrates his pet tremendously. The dog gets trapped in a kind of limbo world. He tries, but is unable to perform like a human being, and loses in some instances even the drive to identify or relate with his own kind. He becomes hostile towards other dogs, refuses to breed or to be bred, etc.

The repercussions of this negative development are even more far-reaching. According to my observations in decades of experience with problem dogs, the breeding of emotionally conditioned dogs can produce a new breed type. Thanks to the puppy mills, this new breed is already flourishing and multiplying. Water-shy retrievers without the desire to retrieve and bird dogs uninterested in hunting are distinct examples.

Is this the result of human arrogance or lack of knowledge? I see the main reasons as misunderstanding dog behavior and misconceptions about the special responsibilities involved in owning a dog. In my opinion, the most detrimental factors in human/canine relationships are:

DETRIMENTAL FACTORS
1. Equality - When the owner sees the dog as "one of the family."
   a. The dog *has* the same rights as humans.
   b. The dog *demands* the same rights as humans.
2. Humanization and catering.
   a. The dog is permanently pampered, coddled, and catered to.
   b. The dog is not treated as an animal, but as a person, which is contradictory to the laws of nature.
3. Double standards, inconsistency, and impatience are combined with unclear, incomprehensive communication and negative training techniques.
4. The dog is not trained at all by the owner and has to self-train. The dog cannot handle this role. Instead of developing devotion, his emotions become incorrectly conditioned. When his emotional and other demands are not being met, he responds with aggression and destruction, and he develops phobias.

CHAPTER 7(M)

Mentally Unbalanced — Dual Standards

Lulu, a nine-month-old cross-breed, couldn't cope with the conflict between her owners, Joan and Dave. Her method of mental escape, however, was different from the typical response of most dogs.

Joan was the disciplinarian. She would not tolerate Lulu in any part of the house other than a corner in the kitchen where her bed was kept. The rest of the time, Lulu spent outside. When Joan was gone, however, Dave would encourage Lulu to join him in the other parts of the house where he even let her up on the furniture. When Joan returned and found the telltale signs of dog hair on the couch, Lulu was severely reprimanded. Joan never knew that Dave was instigating Lulu's behavior.

Lulu managed to hold up against this barrage of hot and cold treatment until she was about six months old. That's when she began to eliminate in the house, even though she had been housebroken since she was three months old. Joan reprimanded her for breaking her habits and began to try and housebreak her all over again. But Lulu got progressively worse, to the point of actually eating her own feces and licking her urine.

Their veterinarian diagnosed the problem (known as coprophagy) as a diet deficiency and prescribed supplements and charcoal tablets. After three months of treatment, Lulu was no better. She was extremely nervous, and along with consuming her feces, she had begun to sleep in it as well. That's when they brought her to me.

Lulu was a pathetic sight; bedraggled, nervous and extremely thin. Although she was left for therapy training, I never worked on her habit of eating feces. Her diet was regular dog food without supplements. I have found that the more mentally and emotionally disturbed a dog is, the more they are inclined to have unclean toilet habits. In milder cases, they tend to step in and walk through their eliminations without noticing what they are doing. Sleeping in the feces and eating them are indicative of more severe disturbances. However, when the mental and emotional aspects of a dog's behavior are balanced through training, they will automatically respond in the physical sense with cleaner habits.

I took Lulu on a one-week trial basis to determine whether or not I could help her. I received a box of various vitamins and a couple of bags of charcoal to mix into Lulu's food. However, it was clear that these supplements did not work and I put them away and did not continue to give them to Lulu. Joan and Dave felt, rightfully so, that the dog did not have a good sense of self-awareness or instinctionally clean habits. Lulu had a history of stepping and sitting in her own feces and would also lie down in it if she happened to be in the area where she had defecated. Because Joan was the heavy-handed punisher, I could not permit my female kennel manager, Mary Ann, to pick up when Lulu defecated or to wash the run down every time she urinated. This became my job. I had my manager check Lulu's run every half hour. If I was needed, I had to stop working and do the scooper/pooper pickup. I tried getting the cleanliness habit across to Lulu . . . and boy, did she start to stink to high heaven.

After about the first week, I finally surrendered and had Mary Ann give Lulu a bath every day hoping this would help to break her pattern. This was only partially effective because in her urine licking Lulu was still engaging in the other part of the behavior. She would squat to urinate and immediately turn around and start licking the urine.

By the tenth day I also realized that Lulu was beginning to develop a flight/fear response whenever I came in to clean or wash down her run. This "keep clean" concept was causing an additional behavior because she must have associated it with Joan's clean up and punish system, which included rubbing the dog's nose in both its feces and urine. This old, out-dated house training method could cause even a stronger, less sensitive dog to become paranoid whenever the owner would approach it, even if it was for feeding or petting. My revised plan of action was "no action at all," to ignore her dirty habits and to just pick up her feces right away.

To transfer the coprophagy habit, I gave her a juicy, meaty bone every day. Also to keep her mind off the habits I scheduled her for 5-

10 minute work sessions every 1 1/2 hours. At the beginning of the day, Lulu was the first dog I trained. She was also the last dog I trained at the end of the day. This first and last training session helped her overcome her emotional responses to human contact. If I walked past her run and saw her engaging in one of her habits, I would take her out for a training session while Mary Ann would clean.

All this extra involvement of both mary Ann and I started to pay off going into the fourth week. At this point Lulu no longer attempted to eat the feces or lick her urine. The owners were called and informed that it was a green light with her rehabilitation program. By the end of the fourth week Lulu no longer would sit or lay where it was not clean. Also when she would walk in her run, I saw her sidestep her feces altogether.

I was pleased to witness this avoidance pattern which she developed on her own and I began to build on it. Rather than have Mary Ann (or myself) keeping the run extra clean, I had her stools left and the run not cleaned at all for one day. This caused Lulu to become more aware where she walked. I began a "clean a day," "skip a day" cycle which created a problem for Lulu because now there was no clean area to lay in the sun. The full length of her run was booby-trapped by her indiscriminating toilet habits. Sometimes when I'm trying to work out a behavioral problem I'll put myself in the dog's head to see how I would respond. Well, Lulu must have done the same because within three days she started defecating only in the rear of her run and off to one side. Once I saw her self awareness and cleanliness habits developing I did not allow her run to get too crowded with her stool, thus preventing her from creating a separation space between her toilet area and her sit/lay in the sun area which she now kept "Mr.(s) Clean."

After the six weeks of therapy training Lulu's habits of coprophagy and licking her urine was broken. She now defecated alongside the cement block wall and in the farthest corner from her water dish and away from where she would lay in the sun.

Her daily training time periods were varied from ten minutes to a couple of minutes to half an hour long. I saw no behavioral changes because of the variables. At the end of ten weeks Lulu was as solid as a rock . . . She had regained her health, weight and peace of mind.

Now the real challenge began — getting the owners to operate on a single standard of behavior with Lulu, and to relate to her with balanced emotions, neither overly affectionate nor overly intimidating. The way I did this was to first demonstrate Lulu's calm and obedient responses to my handling her. Next, we had individual appointments, three private sessions for Joan, three private sessions for Dave. After they had mastered their own rapport with Lulu I had them return as a couple. This permitted each to observe how the other one worked. It has been my experience that by first having separate training sessions with the husband and wife, it prevents any of their marital mother/father roles from interfering with the other's progress in learning. The bonus of Dave and Joan's agreement to a single standard of behavior regarding Lulu was that they created an environment of marital harmony and bliss for themselves.

THE MAN WOULD ENCOURAGE THE DOG TO LAY ON THE COUCH...

CHAPTER 8(M)

IMMOBILIZATION

In most of the behavioral cases I have worked with, a dog either expresses his survival behavior with running away...flight, or attacking...fight. Some dogs with a very low-will and passivity will take action in hiding under the bed or couch to protect themselves from the environment. Out of thousands of dogs I have worked with, there was only one that took a unique course, which I choose to name immobilization. In discussing this case with Dr. Pecci, he commented that many young adults today are "couch potatoes" who remain at home, essentially immobilized, and willing to be totally taken care of by their mothers, while resisting all pressures to force them out of the house to find work. Most of these adults have normal intelligences, but their every need was taken care of by a super efficient mother to the extent that they never developed a strong will or sense of mastery. They felt helpless, and became immobilized at even the thought of entering the competitive outside world. Is it possible that such was the case with Demetrius?

DEMETRIUS

I hung up the phone and wondered whether I should have agreed to the consultation. I had never before worked a dog that couldn't walk.

"I had him checked out by my vet and two specialists from a California veterinarian college in Davis, one a neurologist, and they all came up with the same diagnosis — it's psychosomatic," Dr. Renault explained over the phone. "They couldn't find any physical reason for these . . . spells. I saw in your ad that you do psychological training, so I thought you might be able to help."

"Well, this is a new one on me," I said, "but if you bring him up, I'll be glad to take a look at him."

"Fine, would 11:00 be all right?"

"This morning?"

"Yet, I have to do something for him as soon as possible. I'm really at a loss."

"Okay then, I will see you at 11:00."

As I reflected on our conversation, I began to have some doubts. I had only been specializing in problem and neurotic dogs for a few years and had begun the delicate process of building a favorable reputation for myself in this new field. Had I bitten off too much this time? I pondered the possible causes for such behavior in a dog. It was no use. I'd just have to wait and see the dog. It would take him at least an hour and a half from San Francisco; in the meantime, I busied myself with training other dogs at my school.

The car pulled into the parking lot and stopped. A distinguished-looking man got out of the driver's side, opened the rear car door, and took hold of a leash. He gave it a couple of tugs and out popped a Dalmatian like a cork. I watched as the dog took four or five steps and collapsed to the ground. I went out to meet the doctor. "I hope I am at the right place. Are you Mr. Meisterfeld?" "Yes and yes," I answered, offering my hand. "Why don't you bring him inside?" I stepped back to see how Dr. Renault was going to accomplish this.

"Let's go, Demetrius," he said, smacking his lips several times. He gave a couple of tugs on the leash, but the limp dog regarded him passively and made no move to get up. Finally, Dr. Renault bent down, picked him up and carried him into the office.

After depositing the dog on the carpet, Dr. Renault sat down wearily. It was clear that his concern for the dog had drained him. "What do you think?" he asked. He certainly didn't mince words.

"I think we need to talk some more," I said cautiously. "How old is he?"

"Eight months."

"And how long have you owned him?"

"Since he was about seven weeks old. We bought him from a very well-known breeder in San Jose."

"Did you have a chance to see the sire and dam?"

"Fortunately, yes. They're both perfectly normal — Champions, as a matter of fact. Mr. Fredrick, the breeder, showed me all the ribbons and trophies they'd won for obedience and confirmation. Oh, and they both earned the C.D.X., too. That's what's so confusing to me; with that kind of background, why is Demetrius so messed up?"

"And clinically they couldn't find anything wrong?"

"No." Dr. Renault looked at me expectantly. I wished I had something, anything to tell him. What I needed was time to think.

"I believe I'd like some coffee. Would you care for some Dr. Renault?"

"No, thank you."

I went into the next room and fixed myself a cup of coffee while my mind raced for a clue to Demetrius' behavior. It would have been nice to produce a book and look up "psychosomatic illness in dogs," but at that time, 1967, the field of dog psychology and neurosis was in its infancy. I had only my own experience to fall back on, which was of little help in this case. I'd never encountered anything this serious before. I did, however, have some facts, and through the process of elimination I was confident that I could at least conclude where the problem originated. If Demetrius was clinically sound, and his breeding was also sound, then the problem had to be environmental. With that, I took my coffee and rejoined Dr. Renault in the office.

"Have you done any training with him, Dr. Renault?" I asked.

"Oh, I took him to classes until he started with these spells. The instructor told me to drag him so that he'd be forced to walk. It didn't work, so I picked him up and carried him out and never went back. That suited my wife because she didn't want him trained anyway."

"When does he refuse to walk?"

"It varies. Sometimes when I pick up the leash he's right there, raring to go. Other times, he shows absolutely no interest at all. In that case, he will either refuse to walk or he will collapse later as we're walking. Then, of course, I have to carry him home. Also, at times he forgets his housebreaking. My wife gets livid if I reprimand him. We haven't had so many disagreements since our children were small."

I suspected there was something more to the situation, but further conversation did not disclose anything concrete. "Well, Dr. Renault," I said at last, "all I can promise is that I'll do my best. As long as I can see that he's making progress, I'll continue with his training."

"That's fair enough," he said, and completed the arrangements for the dog's training.

When I was ready to put Demetrius in his run, I took the leash and gave him a couple pats on top of his head. With some encouraging words I started to walk out of the office, hoping he would follow me. He didn't. Demetrius was not tense or fearful, just limp as a dishrag. With as much grace as I could muster, I picked him up and carried him to his run.

After the Doctor left, I went to a peephole, built into the wall in order to view the dogs on the other side, and observed Demetrius. He lay right where I'd left him. About five minutes later he raised his head and looked around curiously; then, unaware someone was watching him, he got up and walked to his outside run. I hurried outside and hid by some grape vines and watched him. Demetrius walked back and forth effortlessly, with no sign of his former disability.

The first week I had no training sessions with Demetrius, although, I'd visit and talk to him for a few minutes several times a day. As the days passed, he began to show some desire for me to take him out, and at the beginning of the second week, I felt he was ready for some training.

I put a leash and collar on him and led him to the ring. So far, so good. I decided to put him through some basics to find out how much he knew. I walked him a short distance and had him sit — at least I tried to have him sit. When his hindquarters went down he would begin to slide sideways. I tried propping him against a wall but he still slid right or left. Finally, I sat him in a corner with his back braced against the two adjoining walls.

Dr. Renault had forgotten to tell me about this problem.

With a little coaxing, I was able to start walking him around the ring. After we'd gone around once, I began to feel there was some hope for the dog. Demetrius continued walking and I was more elated as we began our second time around. I'll have him in shape in no time, I thought. Then my left hand jerked abruptly. I looked down at Demetrius sprawled on the floor — a dead weight. No amount of coaxing would get him up this time. I bent down and began to test his legs for any sign of pain reactions by pinching the flesh. Demetrius flinched so I knew that he definitely had feeling in his legs. There was nothing left to do but carry him back to the run.

I felt discouraged after my short-lived 'victory', so I surrendered to the need for a break. I took a walk down by the pond to try and sort out my thoughts. As I gazed at the rippling water and breathed the fragrant air, I decided a different approach to the situation was in order. I was going to have to watch Demetrius like a hawk and catch him before he staged his act. I also resolved that this was the last time I was going to carry him. The only question was, what to do if he quit in the training ring again? If I just left him there, I wouldn't be able to train my other dogs until he decided to get up. But what if I worked him right in his run? That way when he pulls his act, I could just leave him. Perfect!

The next morning after the runs were washed down, I began Demetrius' training session. We walked the twenty-foot-long run about five times while I was very careful not to pull on the leash. I was not about to justify his refusal to walk. I studied his every movement as my response had to be timed perfectly. As I had expected, Demetrius began to go limp as we walked. Before he had a chance to drop, I let go of the leash and it fell to the cement. Then I just walked out of the run. As I turned around to lock the gate, I glanced quickly at Demetrius, and was pleased to see a bewildered expression on his face as he tottered there. For an instant, he wasn't sure if he should collapse or not. Apparently decided, he fell, and I walked away.

The next session I had with Demetrius, I introduced him to my liverwurst treats. We walked back and forth in his run several times and then I had him sit. The bottom half of the runs are built with concrete blocks and the top half is fencing. I sat him in a corner where the concrete walls gave him support. Just as he'd start to fold, I dangled a piece of liverwurst a few inches from his nose. In response, he sat up to reach the meat. I knew he could not operate on two emotions at the same time. I used the same method when walking him. Anytime it looked like he was going to lag, I'd hold the liverwurst in front of him as we walked to entice him to keep up. I worked him for five minutes that way without him collapsing once. Then I dropped the leash and walked out.

Demetrius followed me to the gate and watched as I locked it. I took out another piece of liverwurst and held it through the fence about two feet above his head. Demetrius hesitated at first, but then he stood up on his hind legs, planted his front paws against the fence and took the treat. It's very important *when working a problem dog to always quit while winning, and while the dog is still eager to work.*

When Demetrius appeared weak and didn't want to work, I cut his sessions down to two minutes. Later on in the week I was able to increase the time to eight or nine minutes. Finally, he was ready to get back in the training ring.

By planning his training sessions meticulously, Demetrius made steady progress from then on. After developing his powers of concentration, we advanced through all the other exercises and commands, including hand signals. In the last two weeks, Demetrius was a willing and eager student, showing no signs of reverting to his former negative habits.

The time eventually came when Demetrius was ready for the first training session with his owners. When Dr. and Mrs. Renault arrived, I ushered them into my office and closed the door. I pulled the window curtains and turned the radio on to drown out any sound they might make. I wanted to demonstrate what their dog could do before they made any contact with him. I knew that once he learned they were there, he'd be too excited to perform the best he could. Demetrius gave a magnificent performance. The couple watched intently as I put him through all the exercises using verbal and non-verbal commands, and off-leash work as well. When I was through, I led Demetrius into the office to reunite him with his owners. It was hard to tell who was more excited, the people or the dog.

"Okay, folks. I suggest we get started with the training session before Demetrius gets too worked up emotionally. I want to avoid any possible setbacks," I explained the procedure to them, then turned the leash over to the doctor. "Any questions before you start?"

"Yes. Do I praise him when he does something right?"

"Not for now. He would probably become too emotional. In the beginning, I suggest using your praise sparingly, if at all. And be sure to correct him gently. We don't want to turn him off or you might end up having to carry him through the exercises." We laughed, but I noticed Mrs. Renault had a dubious look on her face. Dr. Renault followed my instructions well, and soon Demetrius was working proudly for him. "That was wonderful for your first session," I remarked. "Now we'll let your wife have a go."

Dr. Renault turned the leash over to his wife and she took it hesitantly. I thought she might be a bit nervous about working him. "Do you have any questions?" I asked. She shook her head solemnly. "All right, forward."

Mrs. Renault's session was a disaster from the start. She neglected to give the heel command before stepping off, despite my repeated reminders. Worse yet, she consistently got her verbal and hand signals mixed up. After only ten minutes of working him, Demetrius was thoroughly confused and out of control. I called a halt, hoping it would give her a chance to pull herself together. "I don't see why I have to go through all this," she said, flustered. "I don't believe in turning dogs into robots."

Dr. Renault came to my rescue. "Vivian, I like the way Demetrius has changed. Look at him. He's proud and happy, and he walks. Isn't that better than the jellyfish he was?"

"So now that he's cured, why should he have to go through all this? I'm sorry, but I just can't see it. I've had enough." With that, she walked out of the kennel.

Dr. Renault sighed dejectedly. "I was afraid of this. I was hoping that once she saw how beneficial this has been, she would accept it. I can't understand why she's against having a trained dog."

"I'm afraid I can't help you in that department." I said. "But I think you're going to have to work something out for Demetrius' sake."

"Yes, I know. I'll have a talk with my wife and I'll come up with something by next Thursday."

"Good. I'll see you then."

On Thursday, Dr. Renault arrived promptly for his second session, alone. "Well, we've worked it out," he said cheerily, as he came inside.

"Wonderful!"

"Yep, I told Vivian that since it's my dog, I will do all the handling and so on. And she went along with it. I'm even going to build a kennel for him."

"Well, that sounds like a workable arrangement. Why don't we get started then?"

Dr. Renault continued to progress with Demetrius through the rest of his training sessions. The change in his dog was quite remarkable. By the last session he was doing off-leash work, using hand signals only.

"Do you suppose I would be able to show him?" he asked, before taking Demetrius home.

"I think he's just about ready for anything," I said. "He's come a long way and I see no reason why you shouldn't be able to show him. Why, I think he'd even give his parents a run for their money."

"Thanks, Bill. I'm very proud of him."

"Be sure and give me a call after the dog show. I'd like to know how well he did."

"Will do."

I thought a lot about Demetrius in the days following his departure; especially the first 72 hours and the first week. Those are usually the critical periods after a dog goes home in which it's most likely to revert. But since I hadn't heard from Dr. Renault, I concluded that the dog's transition went smoothly.

A little more than two weeks later, I got a call from Dr. Renault. "He reverted, Bill," he said flatly.

I felt my stomach lurch. "Reverted! What happened?"

"I don't know. For the first two weeks he was just perfect. Then about four days ago, he had another spell. I managed to get him up for a few seconds but then he just collapsed again. This morning he defecated in the living room. I thought I'd better call you and find out what I should do."

It was truly amazing how quickly my doubts reappeared. "Why don't you bring him in right now, then I can observe his behavior." And so, Dr. Renault brought Demetrius back and carried him in, just like he had done when he first came. I asked the doctor to call me in two days.

After he drove away, I went over to where Demetrius lay and gave the bobwhite whistle. I picked up the leash and stepped off. There was no resistance as Demetrius got up and walked beside me. After a few wobbly steps, he walked quite normally and I led him to his run and put him in. Strange.

The next day I put Demetrius through his paces for a full half hour. He performed just as he did before he left and showed no signs of reverting. I could only conclude that I let him go home a little too early before. When Dr. Renault called, I made arrangements to keep Demetrius for another week to make sure he was stable before letting him go. At the end of that week, Dr. Renault arrived to pick him up.

"Well, what did you find out?" he asked.

"It's got to be something in the home environment, Jim. Are you using any undue force on him?"

"No. There hasn't been any need to. I followed your instructions faithfully."

I had him work Demetrius for twenty minutes so I could watch how he handled. Everything checked out fine and Demetrius showed no signs of faltering.

"Give him an extra firm snap on the leash, Jim."

He looked at me, wide-eyed. "But . . . "

"I know, I told you not to do that, but I want to see how he reacts. The doctor obliged me and jerked on the leash. Demetrius looked surprised for a moment, but it seemed to wash right over him.

"Well, he should be okay now. Why don't you keep me up to date on his progress when you get home?"

"Okay, thanks again Bill."

Dr. Renault called me every week to tell me Demetrius was doing fine. After the sixth week, I told him there was no need to call me anymore. Satisfied that Demetrius was "holding," I dismissed his case from my mind. Although it's only occasionally that a dog reverts, I usually take it personally, and I'm always relieved when everything works out.

My first call the next Monday morning was Dr. Renault. Demetrius had just gone through another spell. This time I really felt frustrated and had to resist the urge to groan.

"Tell me what happened," I said.

"Well, he was just fine from Monday until Thursday but when I got home on Sunday night, and took him out, he started slipping back."

"You were gone then?"

"Yes, I left town Friday for a lecture."

I was beginning to see a glimmer of light. "Jim, were you on a lecture last time Demetrius reverted?"

"Let me check my calendar and I'll see. Yes, as a matter of fact, I was."

"Who takes care of Demetrius when you're gone?"

"Just my wife."

I didn't need to point out the implications to him. "I suggest you just leave Demetrius in his run and don't work him for a few days. Give me a call on Thursday and let me know how he is. He should be all right by then."

"Okay, Bill. In the meantime, I'm going to have a talk with Vivian. You'll hear from me on Thursday."

Thursday rolled around and I arranged my training schedule so that I'd be available for his call. It came that afternoon.

"Demetrius is fine," Dr. Renault said. "He worked real well this morning. I also talked to my wife about my absences. You know how she felt about the training and all. Well, it seems that when I was gone, she let him stay in the house the whole time. He was up on the furniture, in the bed, and she'd feed him whatever she had for dinner instead of dog food."

"That must be it, Jim. He can't handle two standards of behavior."

"Indeed, I should have connected his attacks with my absence, but it just never dawned on me. I should have talked with my wife a long time ago. If I can't convince her that Demetrius is a dog, he's not going to know it either."

DR. RENAULT BENT DOWN, AND PICKED HIM UP...

CHAPTER 9(P)

CRAZYMAKING

If we observe animals in their natural habitat, we would see that they are usually relaxed and content. So, too, we might conjecture, the natural state of humans is to be happy, loving, creative, and content. Civilizations evolved with the purpose of creating an environment where this natural state would be made possible for larger numbers of people. Yet, the mental state which we encounter in others and experience in ourselves is commonly quite the opposite.

Somehow, we all seem to understand what a person who says, "I feel crazy," means. How do different people describe the experience? It is a state of upset, overwhelm, and turmoil in the head, with no known solution. It is often associated with physical exhaustion, headache, emotional depression or apprehension. The first thing a husband may hear when he comes home is, "The kids are driving me crazy!" And, if the kids had a voice, they would probably retort, "Mommy is driving us crazy!"

Exhaustion can result from overwork without proper rest. However, strenuous activity, when it is exciting, may leave one feeling "tired," but certainly not feeling "crazy," which the old family doctors called "having a nervous breakdown." The cause of feeling crazy is stress, and stress is caused by inner conflict, wherein the mind is filled with unresolved input which creates tension and anxiety. Stress occurs when the innate instincts and the learned, social instincts are at war with each other. There is a paralysis resulting from inner rebellion, guilt, helplessness, and self doubt. This is one definition of neurosis, and hardly anyone is free from it.

The pattern for neurosis begins in childhood. Young children have the extraordinary talent of attuning their minds to the consciousness of the adults about them. If their parents' heads are filled with fear, anger, and worry, the growing brain of the child will attune to this, independent of the parents' words and actions. Thus, children adopt a pattern of moods and feelings from parental figures which can last a lifetime, and which they transmit to their own children. Equally important, each child is born with innate social drives which need reinforcement and positive feedback, if they are not to be extinguished. For example, Harlow's experiments with monkeys and Bowlby's experiments with dogs, raised in an abnormal environment without a nurturing mother and without physical petting, have shown that an irritable temperament and antisocial behaviors are consistent and predictable results. Thus, children who are not hugged grow into adults who do not like to be touched. During the first five years of life, the developing brain is dependent upon environmental input. Sensory organs, unused, may never develop. For example, cats raised in the dark become blind, and children not exposed to speech until the age of six, never learn to talk.

The majority of our children today are raised in abnormal environments. If not directly the target of parental anger and frustration, they are even more crippled by sins of omission. A child needs focused attention, physical embracing, and a loving atmosphere. Books written on self-esteem emphasize the importance of feeling loved in early childhood. Over the years, I have come to realize that even more important than being loved is having someone who appreciates your love. You empower others by how you receive what they have to give. How often do you see little children with their hearts wide open reaching out to give love to a mommy and daddy who shoves them aside, or tells them to stop being a nuisance? The need for a love bond to mommy and daddy is so strong that children, like puppy dogs, persist for years to form one despite repeated rejection. They are made to feel guilty for being needy. And even more devastating, the love they have to give has no value.

What makes a child feel "crazy?" When his head is filled with input that doesn't meld together, and nothing he does is right. Add guilt, suppress emotions, and surround the child with intolerant adults who are so filled with anxiety and fear that they don't notice their effect upon him, and you pretty much have the usual case of what it's like to be a child in our society, today.

We can make mice neurotic (or crazy) in the laboratory setting by giving them the kind of inconsistent feedback which most children experience everyday. For example, we can place mice in a metal cage with a white line on the floor dividing the cage in two. When we want the mice to cross the line, we administer a mild shock to the metal plate on the side where the mice are placed. The mice learn to quickly leap to safety over the white line to the other half of the cage. So long as this is consistent, the mice appear to be minimally disturbed by the inconvenience. However, start administering the shocks randomly and inconsistently, and the mice will soon huddle helplessly in a corner, gradually ignoring the shocks. However, their behavior will be distinctly abnormal and remain erratic for some time after all shocking has ceased.

Let us compare a human situation with a comparable situation with an animal such as a dog. The mother dog rests peacefully until a stranger approaches. Then, the mother dog may bark or snarl until the stranger leaves, when she then resumes once more, her peaceful posture. This is all quite understandable to her puppy, who has no need to deny or repress reality or to suppress its own emotional reactions to this scenario.

In the case of a human infant, however, there is no such thing as mother assuming a restful state of peace, nor is there usually any visible scenario to explain the "craziness" in mother's head, to which the child is attuned. Moreover, the child is at high risk to becoming, unpredictably, a verbal or physical target of a highly stressed mother, with shattering consequences to the child's delicate nervous system. In addition, a child will take each such attack, reprimand, or sense of rejection personally, with devastating repercussions for his or her self concept. Physically, the body becomes armored; the muscles become tense and especially the jaw, throat, chest, shoulders, and pelvis, in an attempt to numb all sensation. But, again, unlike animals, there is no "safe" time in which the child can release this armored guard.

Children cannot gain a sense of significance from parents who, themselves, have no strong sense of significance. Crazymaking in the home occurs when a child is reprimanded for innate behaviors, such as crying, running, curiosity-seeking, and attempting to gain mastery over the physical environment, especially when positive options are lacking. The parents remain depressed or angry and are impossible for the child to please. Guilt, physical abuse, and neglect become introjected into the child's self-image. The home environment of children is filled with anxiety and fear, while unreasonable and inconsistent expectations for compliance are placed upon them. Additionally, mothering from an emotionally depressed woman even though she may mother with good intentions, mistaken in thinking that she is giving love. The presence of a infuses the child with depressive feelings. The presence of a depressed mother in the absence of a strong male presence, makes children irritable, restless, and apprehensive. The lack, in most homes, of a strong and supportive male presence to provide a stabilizing influence, is resulting in a growing population of teenagers who feel no connection to each other or to the established order. In boys, this can lead to the need for affiliation with a gang for a sense of identity, as well as for security. And, the easy availability of guns provides them with the ultimate security blanket. Thus, crazymaking in the home forces the emancipated teenager to seek an escape from their inner chaos and confusion through alcohol, drugs, and sexual promiscuity, while seeking some form of resolution through the joining of cults or gangs.

THE GROWTH OF STREET GANGS

The increasing numbers of street gangs is a symptom of the growing alienation between a significant segment of our young people today, and the social structure. While working in the California Youth Authority, I observed that teenage criminals, who were about to be released back into society, often behaved as if their impending freedom was burdensome, or even dangerous. They were leaving a setting which was safe, predictable, and relatively free from conflict to re-enter a street environment where survival is a predominant concern, where there is a sense of alienation from the greater society, and where they have little opportunity to experience a sense of significance or purpose.

A lack of respect and trust in the prevailing authority structure is usually accompanied by a sense of fear and dread. However, in the extremely stressful and abnormal subculture of street-gang existence, fear no longer serves as a useful ally. Fear, like all powerful emotions, is highly contagious and must be repressed. In its place is seen the cold, callous, unemotional facade of one who has already accepted his death. Those who cannot repress their fear become targets of attack, as if they contained a virus which must not be allowed to spread. The alienation they feel from the outer world, in which they have no real place or role, and the void within their male identity, resulting from an absent father, is resolved by an identification with a small, similarly afflicted subculture as a strictly voluntary act which gives them a sense of freedom of choice.

The seductive aspect is the illusion of choice, that "my fate depends upon me, on my words, on my attitude." In reality, it involves progressive compliance to the gang's values in order to minimize pain and to gain acceptance. By adopting the gang and "choosing" to introject it as one's own world, the sense of intactness is maintained.

The abolition of fear is accompanied by a closing of the heart. There is a lack of empathy for the suffering of others with, often, a paradoxical sentimentality. A teenage gang member may cry at the sound of familiar music or at the death of a puppy. On the other hand, the victim pleading for mercy, may activate feelings within the gang member which he seeks to wipe out through inflicting increased sadism upon the victim.

While animals are feeling-instinctive by nature, humans, alone, are thinking, willing, and feeling beings. Yet, when the feeling aspect, so basic to the animal nature, is insidiously deleted by society, while leaving the thinking and willing aspect intact, then man becomes capable of heinous crimes in both high places and low. It is this capability of the human psyche to put up a barrier between the mind and the heart that makes cruelty so prevalent, and permits even intelligent and psychologically sound people to obediently follow orders to inflict severe pain and suffering upon others.

73

CHAPTER 10(M)

THE DEN INSTINCT

In connection with the "Back-to-Nature-Movement" dog owners were instructed to consider wolf behavior as a model and to imitate the typical wolf behavior traits when interrelating with their dogs.

A specific wolf behavior pattern, which owners were supposed to follow with their dogs, was the "den" instinct — the expression of the maternal instinct of the mother wolf who lives with her cubs in a den.

Dog owners were advised of the necessity to satisfy their pets' den instinct by having their dogs sleep in their bedroom. Dog owners throughout the country readily bought this concept and moved their dogs into the master bedroom. In the past year I have treated several cases of dogs who were providing problems because of their owner's insistence that the dog share their bedroom.

ARNOLD - BEDMATE AND DESTROYER

One young lady, who did her homework first before she acquired a dog, read a best-selling dog book which glorified the "sleep-in-the-den" concept. This became one of her key issues for selecting a certain breed, since the dog had to be large and woolly, so that she could better snuggle with him, and he could keep her feet warm.

Of course, it did not take long before the dog developed quite a few behavior problems. One of them was that he became highly destructive if he was left alone.

When I explained to her that Arnold indulged in destructive activity because of her catering to him and humanizing him, she became very defensive. She justified her habit to sleep under the covers with him by stating that wolves do exactly the same thing. They curl up and cuddle together when they sleep in order to keep warm and express their love for each other.

Try as I may, this was one owner I could not reach and help to understand that her dog had a psychological need for a respected master but not for a mistress, and that she should not use her dog to satisfy her human physical and emotional needs.

THE MERRY BED QUINTET

The following case history shows how close to the extreme the "sleep-in-the-den" concept can be carried.

The couple owned three male dogs and admitted that most of the time all three dogs slept with them. They both enjoyed watching Curley, Larry and Moe pounce around and play on the waterbed.

It seems that the owners had no problems with any of the dogs, except at one particular time of their activity in bed. That was when they made love. The dogs would get so excited by their owners' erotic actions that they tried to get into the act and mimic them. The man found the dogs' sexual intervention quite normal. He stated that he had witnessed this kind of behavior when a pack of dogs ganged up on a bitch in heat. Thus, he found the joining of the dogs very amusing, because he saw himself as the Alpha-dog and pack leader.

The other side of the coin was that the young lady had suffered quite a bit of emotional distress over the whole situation. She was very concerned about the rightness of this practice to sleep with the pack in bed, and the participation of the dogs in the couple's sexual activities.

The woman was somewhat relieved to hear that it was neither natural nor advisable to have the dogs in the bedroom during their intimate times. The bigger problem was the man, because he still believed he should be the leader of the pack. Plus, he enjoyed the exciting action of competing for position. Unfortunately, he carried this "sleep-in-the-den" concept far beyond what the author and trainer's imagination could have conceived.

CHAPTER 11(P)

THE PECKING ORDER

The pecking order, first noted in bumblebees, means that A pecks B, B pecks C, etc. Some form of pecking order has been noted in most social structures, which includes birds, fish, and even insects in addition to mammals. The pecking order does not mean that the dominant male assumes any particular leadership responsibility within the hierarchy. In fact, this is not always associated directly with social behaviors. Dominance behavior is sometimes evidenced as antisocial behavior, probably prompted by the instinct of self-preservation, in over-crowded, competitive environments. Overcrowding leads to many social abnormalities in animals. Crowded rats, for example, display increased fights, hypersexuality, and cannibalism. Crowding almost any two solitary animals together will produce a dominance hierarchy in which one animal becomes boss or kills the other. This is the major cause of death in zoos and aquariums.

This is an interesting thought to ponder in view of the importance which hierarchal systems play in humans. Well-defined and modulated hierarchial systems may be a stabilizing factor to the social order. However, all too often the social desire for personal dominance results in aggressive behavior to establish a higher position in an ever-shifting pecking order. The major theme of some of the most popular TV soap operas in the past decade, such as "Dallas," "Dynasty," and "Falcon Crest," evolves around the continual battling for dominance among affluent and powerful men and women who otherwise appear to have everything the material world has to offer.

In contrast, the dominance hierarchy in social animals, such as baboons, wolves, and birds, is relatively stable from day to day. Conflicts are rare, because one animal will usually step aside to one of higher rank. Interestingly, a female baboon, when mated to a higher ranking baboon, assumes a higher rank. This is also one avenue in our own society by which women rise in the pecking order.

Within the animal kingdom, there are also innate patterns of submissiveness which have the effect of diminishing the aggressive drive of a dominant animal. For example, one pack wolf might offer its throat to a stronger wolf to ward off an attack. This is akin to the advice of "turning the other cheek," purportedly to drain the wrath of an adversary and to check the escalation of hostilities. The overall purpose of the pecking order and of submissive behavior patterns in social animals may be to minimize fighting by establishing a firm, unchallenged hierarchial structure and by diminishing the provocation of aggressive behavior.

Women, regardless of race, have been placed in a relatively minor place in the pecking order in most societies in the world. Even Switzerland, one of the most progressive of democratic nations, did not allow women to vote until 1971. What this means, in a real sense, is that women have had to learn submissive patterns to minimize the escalation of male dominant patterns against them. Most girls learn, before puberty, to adopt "neutralizing" patterns against sexually aggressive overtures. This includes looking away, focusing intently upon something else, maintaining a bland expression, and assuming a hunched, asexual posture. However, almost nothing will work if the girl inadvertently initiated the interest by a long stare, for example. Then the boy will wait patiently for a glance back or a quivering of the lips that will mean to him that a coy, courting game is going on. This can lead to sexual harassment of one type or another, including date rape, and women, until recently, have tended to blame themselves for it.

Every psychologist who works with child molestation and incest must learn to deal with the guilt and shame of the young victim who, somehow, feels compelled to maintain her secret because of a fear of blame. Somehow, the myth of the inability of the average male to control his sexual impulses, has persisted over the centuries and excused men from taking full responsibility for their sexual proclivities. The media contributes heavily to the linking of masculinity and charisma with sexual promiscuity. Sexual activity is a curious human preoccupation unknown in any other living species. It is one instinct over which men are not sufficiently encouraged, or expected by society, to exercise a disciplined mind. Increasingly, rape and other forms of sexual and physical aggression against women are becoming a way in which inadequate men feel free to exercise dominant predatory behaviors seen only in wild animals raised in unnatural environments.

Battered wives learn to become adept at neutralizing aggression by their emotionally disturbed and dysfunctional mates. However, this never succeeds in alleviating abuse indefinitely. In humans, a neurotic distortion of innate dominance-submissive tendencies may result in learned sado-masochistic behaviors wherein the dominant male feels compelled to bolster a shaky ego by repeatedly demonstrating his dominance over a scapegoat who has incorporated satisfying victim responses into his or her personality structure.

In nature, aggressive behavior usually diminishes rapidly when it does not meet resistance. Hence, "playing dead" may offer a salutary benefit. In humans, however, learned aggressive behavior is self-reinforcing, quickly becoming an habitual form of tension release. A milder form of habitual aggressive discharge, all too common in family households, is characterized by verbal abuse including dumping, blaming, humiliating, and threatening to abandon the family. This behavior is almost always a learned pattern from an adult parent or authority figure within the household of origin. In more serious situations in which physical abuse is involved (again, a learned behavior), this may eventuate into an addiction to violence. Once addicted to violent behavior, some men will begin to purposely distort or to misperceive the conciliatory behavior of an habitual target in order to justify attack. And, here, passive submission may only provoke more rage at being cheated of gratifying victim responses. In most cases, this pattern of violent behavior is self-contained within a given household. However, male children who have been victims of, or witness to, this type of emotional release through violent behavior, will often carry this behavior into the streets.

Solutions to the community violence and street violence, which is gaining ever-increasing publicity, should be focused upon supporting the family unit and reducing family violence. And family violence can only be reduced by reducing stress on the male population by assuring them adequate opportunities to provide financial and emotional support to their wives and children. It is a sad fact that inadequate fathers often view their devoted wife and children as adversaries and will attack them for their neediness.

Dr. Carl Bell, an African-American Psychiatrist, writing for the *Psychiatric Times*, May, 1992, states: "Discussions of the 'homicide problem' in African-American communities most often focus on those that occur as a result of predatory violence, interracial homicide, the use of excessive force by police, and gang violence. Yet most African-American homicides result from expressive violence secondary to interpersonal conflict and, as a result, the home, not the street, is the primary location of African-American homicides. Clearly, an individual should have at least one place to feel safe." He adds: "This natural resource, *i.e.*, a loving family, should not be overlooked as a buffer that neutralizes the effects of community violence."

Every stable social structure is maintained by some form of hierarchical system which places each member in a fairly defined place in the pecking order. The more clearly defined the levels and the more available the opportunities to improve one's status within the order, the more stable is the structure, *i.e.*, the fewer the number of conflicts and power struggles and the need for policing.

A good example of this is the military establishment. Each rank has its specific responsibilities as well as its privileges. There is equal opportunity to rise within the system, and equal guarantee of personal rights which insures a sense of significance at every level. There are provisions for health care, food, and shelter which makes this an enticing career path for many, despite the drawback of low financial remuneration. Japanese corporations have operated from a somewhat similar model with much success.

A social system in which there is an almost perfect distribution of labor for the common good is a sponge. A sponge is essentially a large colony of single celled organisms, called protozoans. Some cells can hold on in swift currents, while some can secrete skeletons, and others concentrate on food-getting. This symbolizes something like the kind of social system which the founders of communism initially envisioned, *i.e.*, an equal division of labor for the common good, but its applications to the human condition have obvious pitfalls, not the least of which is the fact that sponges have not evolved significantly over millions of years. Sometimes a society which fills all of our needs can be equally debilitating to our will as one which is indifferent or suppressive of our needs.

A democratic society creates stress because each person is largely responsible for his own survival needs. And, despite constitutional safeguards, equal opportunity for security and comfort is not provided for all, and competition leads to stress which shortens the lives of even the more successful executives of large corporations.

A typical social hierarchy for almost any political form of governing structure might be simply delineated as follows:

King, President, Dictator
Top influential leaders
Privileged class
General population
Underprivileged class.

These strata of relative levels of influence, wealth, and power are difficult to eliminate in practice even in the Republic of Plato or in the socialism of Karl Marx.

It is the nature of people to put relative status upon certain abilities or attributes either earned or gifted from birth. In this country, various surveys have indicated that the status ladder is something like the following:

White
Male
Protestant
Wealthy family
Highly educated
Executive Officer of large corporation
High political position
Special achievement, fame in sports, entertainment, or writing.

At the bottom level of the structure, we might include:
    The homeless
    Mentally unfit
    Welfare recipients and unemployed
    Prison population
    Educationally illiterate
    Unwed mothers
    Delinquent teenagers.

The mistake which most ruling classes appear to have made, historically, which resulted in the crumbling of the entire structure around them, was to ignore their responsibility to the lower strata. Eventually, a tolerance breakdown occurs and pockets of unrest erupt. When these are put down with force, rather than by addressing the problems, they simmer beneath the surface, until they gain the power for a full-blown revolution.

So long as we are dealing with human nature, there is no social structure that can work perfectly. However, almost every social system works best when all of its citizenry are united against a common enemy in times of war. The real challenge comes after the outer enemy has been vanquished and the borders are secure. Then the call for patriotism loses its voice. Now the focus shifts to the inner maneuvering of relative power and status within the various strata of the hierarchy. And the greater the population density, the greater the incidents of conflict. And the external enemy was never as deadly as the enemy within. Konrad Lorenz observes in his classic book, *On Aggression*, that the greatest dangers to every species does not come from the natural enemies of that species, but rather, from those who share the same eating chain. Thus, civil wars have a tendency to be the most bloody, and rioting mobs characteristically seek targets within their own neighborhood.

Dominant Behavior and the Pecking Order

Dominant behavior is more a matter of establishing status rather than aggression. Whenever you question, challenge, or refuse to accept the advice of another person, you are threatening their claim to a dominant status. Children who do this to adults are considered rude. "They don't know their place." Young girls are especially sensitive to comments made about them, such as: "Who does she think she is?" Teenagers, coming into their own power, get into arguments with their parents who refuse to give up their dominance.

Arguments by married couples have little to do with the subject of the argument, and everything to do with trying to affirm a higher status than the other person is giving to them. This mutually destructive pattern has been deplorably adopted by political candidates, who try to persuade the electorate of their own superiority by degrading their opponent. This only succeeds in devaluing both parties and winning votes for "None of the Above." Likewise, sexual harassment in the workplace is more often a matter of establishing dominance than of sexuality.

Dominance is related to relative status within a particular group. It differs from setting to setting, depending upon talents and ties of friendship. Talkshow host, Johnny Carson, acknowledged that he is relatively shy, socially, in contrast to his dominant behavior on the "Tonight Show," where, according to his own words, he "has total control." It is not surprising to see a shy secretary, who works in a legal office, become noticeably transformed during a vacation cruise while she is being served and catered to.

There is a natural tendency, as one grows older, to be drawn more and more to environments which raises one's dominance status and to avoid those which do not. Thus, a successful physician or business-man who does not know how to be a husband or father, will find excuses to work long hours which keeps him away from the family. Workaholics are those who are compulsively driven to engage in an activity which brings them a sense of accomplishment, while avoid-ing their true responsibilities within the context of their family circle.

Dominance behavior in men and women can be measured by the willingness of each to challenge directly the views, opinions, or status of another person. Women do not differ from men in this respect, when they are part of the same peer group, such as attending the same class in college. Dominance behavior has to do more with affirming one's own position, and is only indirectly related to aggressive behavior which involves the active attempt to influence or to control another person for personal gain.

When one's dominance is clearly and comfortably established within a given social structure, there is very little stress associated with holding the dominant position. However, trying to maintain the dominant position in an unstable hierarchy is highly stressful, a risk factor for heart disease in young executives.

The fear of solidly entrenched institutions, political power bases, and of most people in a position of high authority of losing their dominant status if they permit any aggressive expression of a challenge, or of a sign of power from the subordinate or lower classes, is one of the most important causes of social turmoil and upheaval. Certainly, permissiveness might eventually result in a narrowing of the disparity between the two levels in terms of material wealth and privileges, but to the ultimate betterment of both, if done in the spirit of acceptance and respect.

CHAPTER 12(M)

THE PECKING ORDER

Being a pack animal, the dog's social interaction with other dogs, other animals and people is based on the ranking order system, also called "pecking order," in which individuals have to know their place and role in the overall structure, and the whole group follows a leader. Thanks to Mother Nature's creativity and versatility the dog, as an animal from another evolutionary level, has become closely involved with mankind due to the similarity of their social needs and his adaptability and usefulness. Originally, in exchange for work and service, the dog received food and shelter. Man, as the provider, was the recognized superior in this established system. Nowadays, dogs are largely deprived of their original task — to work for us. There are hunting dogs who have never smelled a pheasant or rabbit, herding dogs who never had a glimpse of livestock. Instead, they have become predominantly social companions — pets. This is a very important role too, but contributes to their increasing dependency.

A dog perceives his human family as his pack, and wants his owner to be the respected authority in the top position. Every dog in a human family has the innate need to follow a human leader as a result of his pecking order instinct. For this reason, it is an unhealthy relationship when a dog is treated as an equal. A dog cannot be equal due to the limits of his genetic background and complete dependency on his owner.

The owner should always be aware that the dog's inferior position in this setting has nothing to do with suppression, disrespect or exploitation. It is the consequence of an evolutionary process, as well as a typical behavior pattern of the dog — a completely natural configuration.

Unfortunately, in some man/dog relationships, dogs are not only treated as equals, but as superiors. When an owner does not exercise his head position and responsibility, a strong-willed dog is forced to take over by reason of his "pack/status" instinct. Somebody has to be in charge, and that individual is entitled to express likes and dislikes and to enforce them. The predominant behavior of a highly assertive, strong-willed dog will be demanding and aggressive and his owner has to give in to the challenges and cater to the dog. However, neither the dog nor the owner can be happy in a role contradictory to the laws of nature.

Such a dog becomes more and more frustrated and angry, and when a certain level is reached, needs release and explodes at an object serving as the outlet. Sometimes, the dog will first focus on things, and then proceed to living beings, such as other dogs, other animals, and people (especially children) and turn on them without warning. One day the dog, having spared his owner so far from physical harm, will attack him without the owner deviating from his ordinary routine. The mental overload and adrenal overcharge are responsible.

A dog with a low assertiveness (will to power), who is not able to handle the leader role, becomes emotionally disturbed and more susceptible to physical illnesses. He can show his frustration and dissatisfaction in destructive and annoying behavior, bark excessively, soil the house, run away, etc., and eventually bite as well.

The dog is put into a position he does not want, and negative consequences develop. He is being deprived of what he really needs — a firm structure with man as the master in the center — and the possibility of serving and pleasing him on request on a daily basis, complemented with a little praise and affection for good performance.

Have you ever watched how happy a dog is when he can retrieve a ball or a stick for his master and receives praise for his work? This is truly dog heaven. In comparison, observe the reaction of an idle, spoiled dog when he has to vacate his comfortable place on the couch to a visitor or even his owner.

Nobody can expect a dog to respect a person who permanently caters to him and even treats the dog better than a human being without requesting anything in terms of training or service. The dog feels in a power position and will always manifest his own demands which the owner has to meet because he has become the subordinate.

A dog is only able to understand simple facts when interrelating with his owner in daily life. Are you behaving as my master or do you permit me to be your boss? For a dog it is as easy as that. He cannot comprehend our ideological concepts and motives for human relationships with equality as a predominant component.

A dog does not have our sense of freedom, either. According to our understanding, we assume we are depriving the dog of a paramount natural right if we don't let him run freely and roam for his pleasure. We forget that animals living in the wild never run without reason. They do it for survival. It is detrimental for a pet to be permitted to run uncontrolled. This conditions his primitive instincts and promotes disobedient behavior. In addition, it is irresponsible toward society because of the possible harm to people, livestock, the dog himself, and other animals. Roaming dogs often cause accidents, bite people, contribute to the canine overpopulation, spread diseases, and pollute the environment.

CHAPTER 13(P)

THE SERVITUDE TRAP

In all humans there is an innate will to power coupled with an innate will to serve. The will to power is motivated by the desire to control, gain, own, overcome obstacles and to achieve praise through recognition, status, and power. The will to serve is the desire to admire, emulate, and to follow a strong leader and to gain praise through obedience. We cannot overestimate the urge within the majority of any large population to seek a strong leader with whom to identify and to follow. Almost any strong-willed individual with an unswerving goal and a conviction in his rightness will almost certainly be able to gather some followers about him, regardless of his direction.

The will to serve comes from a genuine desire to establish a positive bond with a strong authority figure, to gain a sense of significance through identification, and to earn praise through selfless obedience.

This type of devotional bond to a person, a cause, or a country brings a sense of fulfillment through service. Every successful politician and every major non-profit organization in this country owes its success to the dedication provided by the individuals who receive satisfaction through serving. Each country is beholden to its patriots for its survival. The search for significance can lead to bonding to a political movement, a cult, or a cause. The willing to serve can be motivated by identifying with an imagined "good," such as a "just" war.

Despite the risks involved, and especially the loss of personal freedom, a common way in which the general masses have chosen to resolve their mutual conflicts, historically, is to subordinate their will to a leader who appears to have all the right answers, and to follow him with unquestioning loyalty. This can lead to fanaticism for a political or religious cause and to radical aggressive behaviors which are resistant to rational reasoning.

There is a world of difference between unconditional obedience based upon mutual respect and trust (*i.e.*, devotional obedience) and subservient obedience attained through the destruction of one's identity and/or will. The first attains willing and enthusiastic compliance motivated by the expectation of praise. The latter attains mechanical servitude behaviors motivated by the fear of reprimand or physical harm. *Subservient behavior is defined as unquestioning compliance or obedience to a dominant figure in the absence of a bond of respect.* It is based upon fear, a sense of hopelessness against all resistance, and a self-image which is compatible with the servitude role.

Every child during the early years from about age two to six, attempts to establish a devotional bond with both parents. These attempts are usually extinguished by father's indifference, or discouraged by mother's refusal to be pleased. Yet, the need is so strong that children will persist until latency years to buy love despite all types of discouragement or abuse. Parents, instead of reinforcing the will to serve, often enforce subservient behavior through threats or physical abuse. This results in power struggles against doing homework, emptying the garbage, or mowing the lawn.

Whenever there is a strong disagreement or resentment against the prevailing authority, and especially one that has the power to make decisions which critically impact our survival, be it parent, boss, or political leader, we invariably will experience a sense of insecurity and inner conflict. There may even be some fear of reprisal should our disagreements become exposed, thus putting us in an open adversarial position in which we are the definite underdog. There is a rebellious streak in most of us, usually kept underground, for the sake of maintaining peace. Most children, for example, will acknowledge being relieved that the adults about them cannot read their minds. Inner resentment and feelings of "it isn't fair," are often suppressed until the teen years when independence is less frightening, and when peer support is available. Some rebellion at this age is necessary and healthy for individuation and need not be of so much concern to parents who are sometimes shocked by the dramatic changes their little boy or girl may go through between the years of 12 and 16.

"Good" little boys and girls who never went through the teenage rebellion, and who insist that they had "perfect parents" are an example of denial. They will often insist that they were loved and respected by their parents, but this was invariably conditional upon their unwavering allegiance to them. This represents the kind of denial the mind will go into when rebellion is not an option, or comes at too high a price. Brainwashing techniques are based upon this principle. Disagreement is made so conflictual and painful, and the relief and the rewards that come from compliance made so enticing, that the mind will go into denial and adopt the belief system that best serves survival.

In primitive societies where the chief or leader is held in high esteem, or in totalitarian societies ruled by an emperor, pharaoh, or king who rules by divine right, the majority of the population avoids inner conflict by adopting the attitude of unconditional obedience.

Undoubtedly, most people born into slavery or servitude status in the past, alleviated their inner anxiety by adopting this attitude of blind obedience. This submissive, non-resistant, servitude mode was often very functional in prolonging survival and in obtaining favored positions of trust in master-slave relationships. The early decision from childhood, of unconditional obedience makes this mode a permanent and predictable attitude, not open to hesitation, or re-decision and hence free from conflict. Dominant behavior by the master of the house is met automatically with subservient responses in order to minimize abusive aggression. The servitude trap is probably unknown in the animal kingdom. Here, we are not referring to merely a pecking order, but to an on-going unbalanced relationship in which one member is consistently benefited at the relative expense of the other. However, the phenomena of victimization, exploitation, suppression of ethnic minorities, and control through intimidation is a characteristic feature of the human condition. Unfortunately, for the human race, women for many centuries and in most countries of the world have been trained by their mothers from birth to assume a

91

subservient relationship to men. Until only recently in this century the family hierarchy was fixed by religious as well as cultural tradition: the man was the ultimate authority figure in the family. His decisions were not to be questioned. In those situations where there was some love and flexibility in the relationship, the woman learned to become an expert in the art of covert manipulation. She might use sex, tears, physical illness, subtle suggestion, or take the advantage of his many blind spots to assume some modicum of control in the situation. However, there were still more times than he knew when she cried herself to sleep at night. Many women who had exhausted all options to maintain some semblance of self-respect, expressed their rebellion by sinking into a deep depression and eventually leaving the physical body, cancer usually being the preferred route.

Battered, abused, and abandoned women constitute the major problem facing our country today. All of the other ills of society come from this because of the deleterious effect of stressed and depressed mothers upon their children. We must not ignore the research which clearly shows that animals raised by mothers in a state of fear or depression grow into asocial, irritable, and fearful adults with poor control over aggressive impulses. This situation regarding the dehumanizing treatment of women is finally beginning to be openly recognized, but is not likely to change dramatically until respect for women is instilled at all levels, the family, the church, the schools, and the workplace.

Subservience to cruelty such as wife-beating must be imposed from birth. And, in the absence of any model of rebellion, it can succeed in suppressing the awakening of the will, and ingrain the subservient behaviors into the self-image of the personality structure. Thus, serfs, scullery maids, and servants of aristocratic lords rarely rebelled, or even considered rebellion as an option.

Abusive parents can have the same effect upon their children. Sadly, I have worked with dozens of fairly well-functioning adults who came from extremely abusive families and who now have no access to their anger. They often present a friendly and happy appearance to cover the inner emptiness they feel. They have difficulty being aggressive in any line of work and often become involved in abusive relationships. Those that are more dysfunctional may fall into heavy alcohol and substance abuse because they were never trained to have a disciplined mind serving a stable sense of self.

What is particularly ominous for the survival of the human race is the current distortion of what Konrad Lorenz calls "Moral Instincts," or special inhibitions against aggression seen in social animals. An animal mother is prevented by special inhibitions from aggressiveness toward her own children. The turkey hen, for example, is prevented from attacking her brood by the inhibition elicited by their cheeping. So, too, infant children have endearing smiles, chortling, and other instinctive patterns to elicit a mothering response. The mechanisms involved are not always clear, but all European breeds of dogs have an inhibitory mechanism preventing them from seriously attacking puppies under the age of seven to eight months. An equally important observation made by Lorenz is that "In animals there is a whole series of species in which, under normal, that is, non-pathological, conditions, a male never seriously attacks a female." He adds, "This is true of our domestic dog and doubtless of the wolf too. I would not trust a dog that bit bitches, and would warn his owner to be most careful, especially if there were children in the house."

The increase of incidents of male violence upon women is an ominous indicator of the progressive mental dysfunction of our male population created by an insensitive educational system, a social structure which provides too few rewarding aggressive outlets, and a television media which distorts the masculine identity by linking it to sexual promiscuity and unrestrained aggression.

A person, reared in the subservient mode, will respond to criticism by going inward with self-blame or self-pity to avoid any retaliatory fantasies which might threaten the relationship. In the concept of "moral masochism," first proposed by Shapiro, a woman may persist indefinitely in her attempts to gain love despite any amount of abuse heaped upon her. Likewise, a well-trained German Shepherd will respond to abusive treatment by its master by licking his hand. Self-concept is so dependent upon the relationships that anger is not a permissible option. When such a person is provoked to the point of tolerance breakdown, the decision will be made, not toward violence but toward capitulation and breaking down into tears, asking for forgiveness, or begging for mercy.

The above scenario is common in some homes in which the insecure man will persist in hostility, provoking his wife, children, or other family members with verbal abuse until they finally break down into tears, an endpoint that usually assuages his violence. In such cases, the man is usually putting the face of his mother on his wife and is punishing her for the humiliation he experienced as a child.

CHAPTER 14(M)

THE SERVITUDE TRAP

Man's Best Friend has been part of the human family for thousands of years. He is the only animal that has an instinctual willingness to work for and serve mankind with unlimited devotion and loyalty. It seems that dogs operate with a sixth or seventh sense when relating to us, as illustrated in the chapter about the dog's devotion and spirituality.

This unique characteristic which separates the dog from all the other species in the animal kingdom, can become a 'Catch 22' when the dog senses a strong emotional need in his master, which he eagerly tries to fulfill. When this need surmounts mere companionship, the dog is forced to function as a human substitute. Because of his innate serving nature and will to please, the dog gets caught in the trap of emotional dependency. A great number of dogs which are used as emotional outlets by their owners have a multitude of problems. They cannot relate normally anymore to their own kind. Although there is no scientific data available, I believe this permanent humanization practiced with generation after generation of dogs is the main reason that various breeds of dogs become increasingly unable to sexually perform with other dogs. As a result, good, healthy male dogs don't get sexually aroused when put in a run with a bitch in season.

I remember two dogs that could only be induced with great efforts to be bred. One was a male black Labrador that would get an erection just when somebody talked to him with a gushy, emotional voice and stroked the top of his head. Yet, the breeding took over 2 hours, because he had to be manipulated to reach his arousal peak and then be physically put on top of the bitch. Several times he would cool off before he got into rhythm and everything had to be started all over again.

Another frustrating breeding situation happened with a female German Shepherd who was flown in from the East Coast. The breeder could not breed the bitch when she was in heat six months earlier. The breeder did not like artificial insemination (which many use today) and hoped with my help it would be possible to breed the dog the "natural way." I had never met a bitch before that resisted the breeding so viciously. It took two of us to hold her still while the stud dog performed. This must have been very traumatic for her. Luckily, the male dog did not need any help and even ignored the threatening, deep-throated growls through her muzzle.

Over the years, I have been witnessing an increasing number of male dogs that get emotionally and sexually aroused just by the owner's voice and by being petted. This is the main reason for my recommendation, "Strokes are for folks, pats are for pets." The stroking is more emotionally charged and reflects the direct physical connection to the emotional state of the owner. Two to three pats contain much less emotional charge. They reflect the aspect of the working and serving relationship our dogs have been originally bred for through the centuries.

One time, when I was a regular guest on a radio talk show in Seattle, Washington, a caller presented me with a specific relationship problem to help him solve. The core of the problem was his girlfriend's doberman. The dog was demanding too much of his time, when he would visit his girlfriend. It seemed to him that the dog tried to prevent them from being too close together, by constantly putting his head between them, when they sat on the couch and watched T.V. When they put Rex in the bedroom, he started scratching on the door and howling. Since this caused too much disturbance in the small apartment for the other residents, they gave him a meaty bone to keep him occupied. Rex was not interested. All he wanted was human contact. When the woman was in the kitchen, Rex was constantly demanding more stroking and petting from the man. My advice was, rather than to cater to Rex and to try to placate him, the next time the dog demanded to be stroked, just to give him two pats on his shoulder and to say "hi" without emotions, just matter-of-factly.

One month later I was informed that this particular caller had already waited on the phone for me for quite some time. He told the listening audience that the first time Rex came to him to demand his attention all he did was to say "hi" and to give Rex two pats on his shoulder. The dog looked dumbfounded and walked away. It worked so well that the dog had not been a pest once for the past month. The man was very thankful, because this doberman had become a wedge in their relationship. He had already considered breaking off his engagement, since he felt he was competing with Rex for his girlfriend's affections and time.

Based on the several thousand dog behavioral problems I have worked with during the past 29 years, I found in nine out of ten cases, when a dog was used for an emotional substitute by his owner, the man usually owned a female and the woman a male dog. This animal polarity of male/female or +/- seems to compound the dog's *servitude trap*. Such was the case in the following story which the owner offered to share so that other dog owners would not put their dogs in this 'Catch 22' position.

CHARLIE
(Gina George's Story)

My story is filled with drama, incident, love and tragedy. Only in as far as the sensational aspects make my message more vivid and memorable do I seek to relate them. This message is directed to the countless women who have doting, passionate relationships with their animals (dogs specifically) and while these bonds can be fully rewarding and deeply joyful and may never come to grief, there will be those that, because of the very nature of these bonds, will move inexorably towards disaster. Mine is such a story.

Charlie is a beautiful black and golden-tan German Shepherd of championship stock who, had he not had his problems, would surely have won some dog show prizes. I wanted a male, I think, for no other reason (at that time) than that I had had a female before and wanted a change. Right at this point I should have stopped and searched my soul. Why did I really want a male? In view of how I thought and felt later, it's clear that I was charmed by the idea of having a male be my protector. Not that Lisa (my other dog) hadn't protected me, but we know that males are supposed to be the true protectors. I was probably responding to some inner prompting which urged me as a female to find my male defender. "Me Tarzan, you Jane!" Why a human male couldn't take on this role (though I was attached to one) is unclear to me. Could it be that tradition is losing its hold in view of the new push towards equality between males and females?

Anyway, I picked a male, and not only faulted on this, but I picked him because he was quiet and withdrawn instead of friendly and scrappy like the other pups. I thought his behavior was sweet, and it inspired the mother instinct in me to protect and shield "my baby" from the scary world around him. Little did I realize that this protector and baby, aided and abetted by me, was going to play out his role to the hilt!

It's not as though I didn't have fair warning. Two days after I brought him home, he responded aggressively and fearfully when handled by the veterinarian. The doctor promptly told me that, if I weren't too attached to him already, I should give him up, since Diskin was "neurotic and paranoid" and when he grew up he would cost me a great deal of money to train. But giving him up was out of the question. I was already in love. I was determined though, to bring up my dog so that by the time he became a teenager, I wouldn't have a brat, or a criminal-minded beast, but a loveable, well-adjusted dog.

So I began my efforts diligently. I would be very disciplined at first, then I'd slowly, slowly peter out. This weakness really was the crux of all my problems, and something which I believe I share with many, many others. The fact is, I wouldn't — couldn't — follow through with my disciplinary measures. I simply lacked discipline myself and if *we* lack it, then no matter how we are motivated, by love or whatever to achieve our goals, we will not succeed. It seems almost trite to be restating something that has become almost axiomatic and yet it appears we need to be reminded again and again. Sometimes I suspect that the only way we acquire discipline is through the severe consequences of our actions. But I'm jumping ahead a little here. As I said, I set about trying to cure my pet of his fear of people. For example, we'd go and spend time at the bus-stop where there were lots of people bustling about. Not much success though. He would always be hiding behind me or burying his head under my arm so that he wouldn't see or be seen.

Then came time for First Grade. We went off to school together once a week to learn how to do all those good things dogs are supposed to do. Sure enough, Diskin excelled in class. He did everything perfectly. But when we got out, guess who was pulling whom around! And he was getting pretty strong, too. At first we practiced everyday, then one or two days would go by before I'd try again. In the meantime I pampered, coddled and loved him without restraint.

One day when he was a little over one year old, Diskin's brattiness took a really serious turn. We were walking when he spied a little boy further up the hill. Promptly Diskin took off after him. It was luck and quick reaction on the child's part that saved him from getting more than a nick on his arm. I reprimanded Diskin severely. He was crestfallen and shamefaced; he hadn't really meant to do it but "you know how it is, Mum, I just lost control . . . " Well, we took off for Mexico anyway, as planned, that same day. Bill Meisterfeld (who was later to take him in hand) pointed out that this was quite a mistake. It was as if I were rewarding him by immediately taking off in the car (which he loved) on a long trip.

Six months later, the inevitable happened again, only this time he bit a man in the seat of his pants, who was trying to save his cats from being attacked by Diskin and some other dogs. It was now quite apparent that I had a real problem on my hands. I could never trust that he wouldn't simply dash out after someone, and if he were on leash, it was a question of my strength against his. He'd become in short, quite unmanageable — a spoiled "child," but never, thank God, a truly vicious dog. His underlying problem was that he feared people and this manifested itself in cowardly attacks on creatures who were either weaker or at some disadvantage. The trouble was that in time he could very well become more plucky and do some real harm.

Diskin was one and a half years old when Bill Meisterfeld came into his life. During the five months that Bill had him, he made Diskin work like a dog. Every day he learned and relearned what his limits were. His world was defined for him, his position in it, and how this related to his master. At the end of those five months, Charlie Brown (we'd changed his name so that it would take him down a peg or two in my eyes) came home transformed. I'd also changed, supposedly. I'd gone to ITP to reeducate myself so that I wouldn't pamper, coddle and smother my dog with love. I would be the master. Charlie wasn't going to run all over me, etc., etc.

So it was that we happily started out on this new path. Everything went fine for a while. Charlie slept outside in a kennel instead of on my bed. I refrained from kissing and otherwise expressing my love, and we did our lessons everyday. Then the dam burst. It was torturous for me not to demonstrate my love. I could not give this love in measured doses. The nature of my feeling demanded expression — extravagant expression. It was impossible — those limpid, beguiling, brown eyes would melt my heart, and he knew it. He had an arsenal of charms to bombard my defenses, and he used them mercilessly. He was always a great cajoler, and I must confess, I loved being manipulated in this way. But when this emotional dam burst, lo and behold, Charlie was able to handle it, give it back in full measure and still be an obedient dog. Bill had done an excellent job, and charlie had too. he could have reverted, but didn't. Somewhere in his psyche, Charlie had decided that he wouldn't let his mistress garble up his life. At least as far as his relationship with people went. During his time with Bill, he learned to let go of his fears, and he came around to learning respect instead. And so it is that I'll never have to worry about Charlie biting again. Thus ends this chapter of Charlie's life — happily. But my lack of consistency as far as discipline was concerned, was still to rebound on me with a cruel and final lesson.

It happened in Los Angeles one and a half years ago. Charlie was four. I had kept up his training as far as heeling and sitting went. I was afraid he would be struck by a car, so (during the day) these commands were always in force when we'd come to curbside. Night was another matter. On beautiful balmy evenings, I'd take walks and would become lax with my commands. It came about that he would walk and run quite freely across those deserted side streets without a word from me. I wasn't afraid; after all, there were no cars around.

On that fateful night, Charlie had been on his leash, and I had just turned him loose to do what he had to do before we turned in, when he saw a dog about a half block away across the main street. Boom, he was gone like a shot, and as he crossed the street he was struck. He could have died right then and it would have been a fearsome lesson to me, but I wasn't going to be let off so easily. Both his back legs were injured; one leg was broken, the other dislocated.

Three weeks later, Charlie's life was still hanging by a thread. Infection raged, and I was beside myself with the horror of it all. Charlie's only hope was the veterinarian school at Davis, California. Four months went by. Four months of hope, despair, renewed hope and finally he was released a three-legged dog, suffering from a bad case of muscle atrophy in the third leg. The bill was upwards of $4,000, and I had experienced much, much anguish — not to mention Charlie's pain. it has been a full year since his release. I will never have to worry about his dashing out into the street — he simply cannot move very fast anymore.

We women who own dogs, especially if we're single, can fall into a dangerous trap when we love our animals madly. Because they're "only dogs" we often give full reign to our mothering instinct, our need to feel protected, our emotional love needs. We wouldn't treat a child this way, after all he might grow up emotionally disturbed. Then why do we so conveniently forget, and treat our animals this way? I know I can't answer this — I'm one of the culprits. Even so, there is something deeply satisfying for me in being able to give full vent to my love feelings with my pet. The relationship becomes deep, complete and joyful. The fact is, there are relationships that no matter how deep, how emotionally charged, the animal remains sane, healthy and obedient. My old dog Lisa is a perfect testimonial to this. Even Charlie has shown amazing adaptability and recuperative powers. In so many ways they are like us!

Theoretically, we're all capable of so much more, but in practice, again and again we fall short of the ideal. So my message is, in essence, be aware of your desires and limitations and choose your future pet based on this knowledge of yourself. This means, referring back to me as an example, *no more males!* I recognize this subterranean desire was the root of much of my trouble. But as far as my inability to be a consistent and thorough trainer, I think I've actually undergone some profound changes. In the future, consistent discipline will be a must. It's funny, but in view of what has happened to me, maintaining discipline won't be something I *have* to do, but something I *automatically* do, like breathing and eating — to live.

It is tragic — we speak of the wonders of achievement through discipline, but there's nothing that teaches us so well the value of it as in the harsh resultant experiences of our actions, otherwise called Karma.

CHAPTER 15(P)

POWER STRUGGLES

All of us have experienced being on one side or another of a power struggle at some time in our life. In fact, some people believe that power struggles are an unavoidable part of every relationship. Who's calling the shots? If they are trying to do it without agreement, then there's going to be a hassle. Even when there is a designated authority figure such as parent, teacher or supervisor, the ongoing struggle to maintain power and control against covert and overt opposition seems interminable. I have been called in as a consultant many times in all of these situations.

Parents come to me complaining: "I can't get him to obey, no matter how hard we punish him." Teachers complain, "I don't have time to analyze his family background, I just want him to stop disrupting the class." Executive officers of large corporations want to know, "How can I improve morale? How can I get these people to follow orders without dragging their feet?"

Power struggles evolve around the issue of control. They result from a lack of a clear-cut delineation of roles, or a lack of respect for the designated authority figure. Power struggles manifest in a number of ways, from overt rebellion against all control to more subtle expressions of defiance, including harassment and partial compliance, which frustrates the authority figure.

Even power struggles are learned behavior. Children, for example, learn to capitalize on the weaknesses of a parent to resist control. They quickly sense the parents' guilt, self-doubt, lack of clarity, and need for acceptance by the child. This allows them to get away with slow, impartial compliance or even total disregard for rules. These energy draining power struggles can make a nightmare out of parenting and teaching the young, and yet they are totally self-created by the person in authority.

A power struggle may be defined as a battle of wills between a person in a designated position of authority and a subordinate. In the usual case, the authority figure attempts to maintain the power position by utilizing considerable energy in the form of force, threat, bribery or punishment to enforce compliance.

The resistance may take on many forms and may range from subtle and covert to outright rebellion. Authority figures expect their wishes to be carried out either through willing compliance or else by enforced control. Willing compliance is only attainable in an atmosphere of mutual respect and trust between an authority figure and a subordinate. When this is lacking, then a power struggle will eventually arise out of the issue of control

Parents are notorious for inflicting their wills upon their infant children in a controlling manner which arouses anger and resistance. Anger is the natural biological response to enforced helplessness, fear, humiliation, or a felt attack upon self-concept.

For example, any sudden disruption of the natural flow of an ongoing activity, whether it be motoric play, exploratory curiosity, or pleasurable exercising of the five senses results in a blockage of energy that leaves a sense of incompleteness, and evokes an inner protest. The more frequently barriers are imposed to natural expression, the greater the build-up of frustration, especially in the absence of clearly defined acceptable activity. Thus, a series of insensitive No's, imposed midstream on an already initiated activity by an intolerant parent, can push almost any child into a temper tantrum. This is an example of overt control by the parent in which compliance is attained by intimidation or physical force. Note that willing compliance might easily be attained if the parent became sensitively involved in the activity and then redirected it into a more acceptable area without damming up the energy.

As the child grows older, shaming and guilt are common means of controlling the initiation of unwanted behavior. The fear of upsetting a brittle parent and then being made to feel totally unworthy of love is a major deterrent to the spontaneous expression of any emotion or activity.

Children have an innate need to please and to gain acceptance. Any behavior that brings a response of praise or an expression of love will be compulsively repeated over and over again. And we too, like children, also get a sense of personal power and self satisfaction which is dependent upon our ability to please or to impress others. There is no one more important to a child, no one whose praise is more valued than that of a parent.

Every parent has all of the advantages over their child that they could possibly need to guarantee blind obedience, namely awe, respect, dependency, and a need for love and a desire for praise. Yet, sadly, all too soon they lose respect and trust by needlessly attempting to enforce obedience through reprimand, coercion, punishment and guilt. When a parent is impossible to please, the child feels powerless, and may give up trying to earn love. Once a child feels unloved and that his own personal needs are not a high priority, his willingness to obey the wishes of a parent markedly diminishes. This only reinforces the parents' attempts to control by breaking the will, seeking subservient behavior rather than willing behavior.

Reprimand and punishment only alienates the child from the parents. It instills a negative self-concept that is no longer capable of earning love. Control of behavior through coercion and guilt arouses inner rebellion and defiance. A vicious cycle occurs in which the angry, hurt, and humiliated child engages in a variety of power struggles with the frustrated and emotionally drained parent who intensifies attempts to break the will of the child through increased punishment and threats.

The pattern of power struggles learned in the home is carried over into the greater community. Thus, the integrity of the family unit becomes the core strength of any great society. Power struggles represent a breakdown in discipline which results from a lack of respect for the person in the authority position. Punishment, then, becomes necessary to maintain control. The need for excessive physical force or violence to maintain civil control always signals the beginning of the end of the regime in power. The polarities have widened beyond repair and the pattern of defiance is now clearly established.

The Vietnam War is a case in point. Prior to this, it was almost unthinkable to resist the draft or to oppose a war. But here there began a gradual distrust of the motives of our national leaders and in the manner the war was conducted. Once protests began, primarily by students on college campuses, they spread rapidly. The use of violence at Kent State marked the beginning of the end of public support for the war.

This power struggle arose from an attempt by the ruling authority to maintain control by suppressing the free expression of criticism. Paradoxically, in a democratic society, the opportunity to speak out lessens the likelihood of rebellion. Similarly, an experienced parent is able to handle a toddler's assertive No's in a benign, non-suppressive fashion. By acknowledging the feelings of the child, the parent conveys the sense of significance the child is seeking, and this quickly dissipates the motivation for defiance.

There are a few important prerequisites for attaining compliant behavior. Any individual's behavior is highly dependent upon the structure of the setting and the quality of the authority figure in charge. An environment that is properly structured to encourage compliant behavior, whether it be the home, a classroom, an office, or a prison setting must provide positive answers to the three basic survival questions in order to minimize power struggles:

Survival Questions

(1) *WHO AM I?* The individual must be able to identify with the person in authority in terms of respecting the authority figure's goals and responsibilities, while simultaneously feeling valued themselves as someone whose basic needs and rights as a human being are respected.

(2) *AM I SAFE?* Is the society or person in authority sufficiently strong and willing to be responsible for ensuring my safety from physical abuse, harassment, and victimization by anyone else sharing the environment? Will my personal boundaries be respected? Will reasonable accommodations be provided for food, water, clothing, and other basic survival needs?

(3) *CAN I COPE?* Will the expectations upon me be reasonable and consistent and will opportunities be available to maintain a sense of significance by being allowed some form of personal expression and recognition?

No person or group can function optimally in any setting until these three questions are appropriately resolved. And each setting has its own set of answers. Thus, a child who has problems at home may be a model student in school, and conversely, a disruptive student may be a leader on the basketball court. This means that every authority figure, given the proper support system, must be personally responsible for the behavior of those placed in his charge.

A true leader has the respect, trust, and devotion of followers which enables him to lead them through sacrifices and deprivation without resistance. On the other hand, most dictators maintain control through fear, intimidation, punishment and oppression. The energy of constant vigilance needed to enforce compliance under those conditions will ultimately drain the resources of his country.

At the other extreme is the weak leader or the insecure parent who uses catering to be accepted and liked and bribery to buy cooperation. This creates a major shift in the motivational energy of the child or a subordinate from one of seeking praise to one of feeling manipulated. The catering and the bribery becomes an expectation and then soon becomes a demand, and the price keeps getting higher. No one is more disliked than a leader who is afraid of his responsibility. A strong leader may not be liked, but might still be respected and his orders followed without question, provided they serve a common good.

If the fear of punishment is the only incentive for compliant behavior, eventually a tolerance breakdown may occur in which the consequences have lost their meaning. This can lead, on a family level, to a battered wife shooting her husband and, on a national level, to revolution or anarchy. Anarchy, a state of total social upheaval, only occurs in the absence of a respected leader or loss of faith in the political system. The fear of mob rule, which inevitably fosters uncontrolled violence, has led past populations of republics and democracies to elect, out of desperation, a dictatorship in an attempt to maintain order through unrestrained power. This is the challenge that faces the new democracies of the former U.S.S.R. today.

CHAPTER 16(M)

CONDITIONING THE TWO WILLS

Every dog (and child) has an innate will-to-please or serve and a will-to-power. The will-to-power and the will-to-serve ratio is present to a different degree in each dog (and child) at birth. This ratio can be dramatically changed and even reversed by environmental conditioning. When the will-to-power exceeds the will-to-serve, we have a potentially dangerous dog on our hands (see pages 130 and 131).

Graph #1 shows a characteristic pattern of what normally happens when a domestic dog is left untrained. The will-to-power gradually rises while the will-to-serve becomes extinguished. By 14 months — the "teen rebellion" age of dogs — its behavior suddenly becomes very independent and it will likely refuse to come when called, and may growl when told to get off the bed. Now, aggressive handling is likely to be countered by comparable resistance. Because it has not been trained to have a disciplined mind, it may initially evidence insecurity until, with increasing maturity, it becomes more assertive and may develop destructive biting behavior.

Graph #2 depicts the pattern that might be expected of a dog with a similar personality make-up (i.e., will-to-serve level 7, will-to-power level 5), but who receives emotional humanization (i.e., child substitution), placating, and being catered to. This promotes an accelerated rise of the will-to-power and a more rapid decrease in the will-to-serve. By the age of 7-8 months, it may demonstrate the aggressive behavior of an older "teenage" dog. Now, if catering continues, by the age of 15-16 months, it will very likely be totally unmanageable. It may be destructive to the home when left alone and, if displeased, is literally capable of biting the hand that feeds it.

Graph #3 is an example of a dog with a similar personality make-up to dogs 1 and 2, but who received psychological obedience training based on a bond of mutual respect with its master which enhances the will-to-serve. This conditions the disciplined mind so that behavior problems do not arise. The will-to-power is allowed to develop normally, but remains governed by the will-to-serve which is under the control of its own disciplined mind. The disciplined mind uses discernment, and is non-reactive to the environment, but responds instead to an inner idealized model of behavior which overrides the adrenal rush. This "idealized model" comes from devotional obedience to a respected authority, and maintains a steady, consistent level of behavior even in the absence of that authority figure.

Graph #4 depicts what normally occurs when a dog who has an exceptionally high will-to-serve and a normal will-to-power is trained by the alpha dominance method to offset the disobedience which appears to work for about 30 days, during which time the owner continues catering behavior. Now the dog's self-assertiveness/will-to-power again attempts to take over, and again is beaten by the owner into submission with the belief that the owner's dominance needs to be periodically reinforced. Each time the will-to-power is suppressed by force, *there is a simultaneous depression in the will-to-serve!* This pattern occurs approximately every month, each time requiring greater and greater force to combat the dog's increasing resistance to submit. Meanwhile the dog's will-to-serve drastically declines to a point where the dog will not absorb any more abusive handling. This constitutes a tolerance breakdown, in which the dog will no longer submit to any previous supposedly effective dominance training methods. At this point the dog is usually labelled unpredictable and dangerous "due to a genetic defect."

These graphs take on an even more profound significance when we consider the parallels between dog training methods and the accepted training practices to which young children are commonly subjected.

CHAPTER 17(P)

THE PERFORMANCE TRAP

Why is it that humans are not more happy? Why is the human condition so beset with fear, turmoil, and overwhelm? It isn't that we don't have intelligence. Humans have been gifted with a brain that has allowed them to dominate all other life forms on this planet. Perhaps, it is because of the direction we have chosen to focus our consciousness. Human beings are caught up in the endless search for significance through performance, by being driven to attain more admiration, more praise, or more wealth than anyone else. The major contenders drive themselves to keep pursuing this elusive goal by stoking themselves with guilt, self-reproach and blame. Reaching a materialistic goal in our society has become more important than how you get there.

Each society puts its own value judgments on what attributes or talents are to be praised and rewarded. In ancient Greece, for example, a philosophical thinker might be held in esteem, whereas in ancient Sparta or Rome, a sturdy and fearless warrior might be the popular choice for awards. We might assume that during the Renaissance period in Europe, musical and artistic talent gained high recognition, as did literature and poetry in Elizabethan England.

Today, artists and poets, with rare exception, are not a thriving profession. For the past 50 years, increasing value and emphasis has been placed upon a test measurement developed in the early part of this century called I.Q. This, essentially, measures the capacity of the left brain to act like a computer in storing, retrieving and analyzing words and symbols. And the speed at which it does this is of prime consideration in the scoring. It does have its value if its limitations are recognized. It does not attempt to measure the creative, artistic, intuitive talents generally attributed to the right brain, and from which all of our noblest achievements in music, literature, and scientific discoveries have come.

111

The push for scholastic performance begins at an increasingly early age. With this is the promotion of competition for technological skills which gradually closes down the right brain and, with it, an identification with nature and spiritual values. The outer world becomes more real than the inner. We are taught in school, the first time we are old enough to be in a spelling bee, that there are winners and losers. In our school system, the name of the game is competition. Grading is often based upon a curve. Students are tested and re-tested to meet state and national norms to justify the administration of the school system. Basically, this shows who is best at short-term memorizing of reams of rote information and regurgitating it upon demand in a prescribed way. The same small group of students keep winning all the awards, medals, honors, and scholarships. Those who win are not to be envied. Success has its own special trap. The win is exhilarating, but temporary. The need for an encore begins immediately to re-establish proof of significance by beating the old mark.

A sad example of this is illustrated by one of my friends in high school, whom I shall call David. David was an over-achiever who won almost every academic contest he entered. I both admired and envied him. Initially, we were competitors, but it soon became clear to me that there was no contest because I was either unwilling, or unable to discipline myself to invest the energy he was willing to put into winning. He maintained a 4.0 average and was also a gifted cello player. In our junior year, he won the state spelling contest against all other high school contestants. That evening, he called me on the telephone to announce his success. I did not recognize, at the time, that he was not meaning to be boastful, but rather, was making a desperate attempt to reach out for love and respect. The high school principal called a brief student assembly to acknowledge the honor he brought to our school. Yet, only in retrospect, do I realize how lonely he was. Other students tended to ignore or to resent him.

After graduation, David went to Yale and I never saw him again. However, I did receive a newspaper clipping from him a year later which had appeared in his hometown paper, acknowledging that he was the top student in the freshman class that year. A couple of years later, I inquired about him to a mutual friend. He answered, "Didn't you hear about David?" On a trip to New York City, David had slashed his wrists and jumped from a ten-story building.

This had a profound effect upon me, as if David had fallen victim to a form of disease which I, myself, had narrowly missed. As a psychiatrist I became interested in treating suicidal adolescents. From my own work, and from reading the literature on teenage suicides, I came to see that David's case was not unique. It is often the highest achiever, the most successful and gifted high school student who suddenly takes his life. I have interviewed many who seriously attempted suicide by various means but had failed.

Each talked about their sense of overwhelm, their inability to keep up the competitive pace, and the despair of what they faced ahead of them in maintaining a high status level at the major college which their father had selected for them. Brian is a characteristic example. He was referred to me after he calmly and without much prior thinking about it, decided to take ten of his mother's sleeping pills before going to bed. He did not even leave a suicide note because he wasn't quite sure what to put on it. He was surprised to wake up the next day, because he had underestimated the lethal dose. He then told his mother about the attempt, which prompted his referral to me. Brian was not enthusiastic about talking about the incident. He was more apathetic than depressed, and somewhat disappointed that the suicide attempt had failed. He stared at the goldfish in my fish tank and stated: "Why can't life be like that? There's no pressure on them to do anything." Brian was scholastically at the top of his high school class and was also a top-ranked tennis player. But life, for him, was insipid. He felt alone, confused, and directionless. His father was largely absent, attending his law practice, but would occasionally come to see his tennis matches. He was being pushed for a tennis scholarship at Stanford, but he had met some of the gifted players in the national high school finals who planned to attend Stanford, and he dreaded the work it would take to maintain their level of competitiveness. He had come to realize that he was only doing it to gain his father's love, and that, somehow, it all wasn't worth it. I do not have the statistics on this, but I have never met a suicidal teenager or even a delinquent teenager who had the love of a strong, supportive father figure in the home! A large percentage of homes in our country today have the absence of a strong masculine presence which affects adversely the mother as well as the children. What this signifies to me is that the war on drugs, the war on crime, the war on school dropouts, and the war on street gangs and violence must begin, and cannot be won without, the establishment of a responsible fathering role for all men in our society.

It might come as a surprise to consider that teenagers, as a group, are the most alienated from society. They serve no useful role or purpose. From early childhood and throughout the most vital and creative period of their lives they have been warehoused in sterile square rooms with 30 or more other students, and fed an endless stream of information that is completely irrelevant to what is really going on in their lives, in their homes, and in the streets where they live. They are offered little or no opportunity to find a sense of significance based upon a meaningful role in society. The most dehumanizing aspect of segregating 30 boys and girls in one room is that children are not homogeneous either in size, looks, rate of maturation, or modes of learning. Some children are visual learners, some are auditory learners, and a significant percentage, mostly boys, are motoric learners which means that they have difficulty encoding information when their hands are not actively involved in the input. They tend to be restless, become behavior problems or daydream their way through the day. They feel like misfits and have a strong dislike for school. Similarly, the primarily right-brained children are forced to limit themselves to the more tedious, less satisfying mode of linear learning of rote information.

Put yourself into the head of almost any teenager today and you will find little sense of personal power. Instead you will find confusion, insecurity, a sense of isolation, and of alienation from society, and frustration at every level due to the blocked expression of pent-up aggressive, emotional, and sexual energies. Behind it all is a deeper spiritual hunger which is not permitted to be addressed by the school system.

The comparison and competition that is taught in our schools carries over to the adult work world in which a pattern of never-ending struggles to raise or maintain one's position in the pecking order results in burn-out, apathy, wanting to give up, and chronic depression. Those caught in the performance trap are compelled to seek for money, power, fame, admiration, and praise as substitutes for love.

The value placed upon the three-dimensional world is such that one's identity becomes synonymous with physical appearances and possessions. By becoming identified with performance, people become entrapped in an isolated area of relative excellence so that the quality of life is lost. Enrico Caruso said at one point in his life that he felt trapped by his voice. People, everywhere, wanted to hear it and he had to go along.

The loneliness of the wife of the male achiever is legend. A man's self-concept becomes tied to a limited area in which he excels and upon which he may base his entire identity. I know of many quality physicians who spend long hours in surgery and in patient care and hospital visitation to the neglect of their family because they feel a greater sense of importance, and have a more clearly defined role, in a hospital setting than of a father or husband in the home setting. In this, however, the quality of life is lost through demanding and unsustainable performance that often shortens life.

The anxiety over performance can even take the enjoyment out of sex as illustrated by a disclosure made to me by one of the charismatic student leaders of the 1960's Free Speech Movement who found himself pursued by numerous women who saw him as an outspoken, arrogant, masculine sex object. He confided to me that he had been forced into celibacy because he was afraid of being unable to perform according to expectations, and he did not want word to get around that "JR is a lousy lay."

Nothing captures an individual in the dehumanizing performance trap more than success. Japan is an excellent example of the performance trap resulting in a high rate of teenage suicides. Once,

115

one of the most artistic and creative people in the world, they have shifted almost entirely to their left brain, becoming transformed symbolically into hamsters turning a giant money wheel, with no time off for rest on weekends or holidays. Meanwhile, they berate the United States for "being lazy," which really means that we are not as driven into putting so much time and energy into pursuing a sense of significance which takes precedence over pain, pleasure, or even long-term physical survival.

I have treated a number of intelligent, talented and attractive young adults who are so stressed by their highly competitive work situations that they are relieved to escape to the solace of their barren apartments each evening rarely socializing or taking the time for recreation. In their escape from the stressful world, they have become unaware of how lonely and sterile their lives really are.

FLOWER CHILDREN OF THE 60's

My psychiatric residency in the early 1960's at Langley Porter Neuropsychiatric Institute, next to the University of California Medical Center, in San Francisco, was an almost perfect timing and location for me to study the new phenomenon of the growth of "Flower Children," or "Hippies," who were becoming increasingly entrenched in the nearby Haight-Ashbury District of The City.

The initial influx consisted of largely middle class and upper middle class young adults who were seeking an alternative to the successful and affluent life styles of their parents. Their own lives had been comfortably carved out for them in the established order, to succeed their fathers in a lucrative business occupation. It was no coincidence that the Hippie phenomenon began with the discovery and general use of drugs, such as LSD. I enjoyed mingling informally, on the street corners with this friendly population, out of a natural curiosity to explore the motives that had driven them to this kind of existence. Although they did not all state it in exactly these words, many of them openly shared with me that, as the result of a hallucinogenic experience, they were able to gain a higher perspective of consciousness and of life, and could see the shallow existences their parents were living behind a sham of pretense. The hallucinogenic experience offered them insight into the world of their parents' which was a highly predictable and mechanical existence that was essentially devoid of any real love or real happiness. Little time was set aside for the precious moments of inner atunement and the contemplation of the meaning and purpose of life. They were trying to express that their parents, in the wild pursuit of establishing social esteem and success, rarely appeared to be at peace with themselves. This was evidenced by the fact that it didn't "feel good," to be around them. It was as if they had "no place of peace to go to" in their heads.

These young adults who were being preened to follow in their parents' footsteps, were, instead, trying to "feel good," even if it meant "spacing out." A few of them articulated words such as seeking "inner wisdom," or, "higher truth," however none were really sure where they were going. They were only clear that they wanted to change the direction in which their parents were pushing them. They were able to see that their parents were living a life of pretense: over-stressed fathers pretending to be in total control, and depressed mothers pretending to be happy. It was not a pleasurable experience to converse with them because they were so out of touch with their true motives and feelings that all they had to offer were pithy aphorisms. In contrast, there was a real sense of significance to them in the greeting statement which eventually became a trademark of the Hippie subculture: "Say it like it is, man."

THE CORPORATE TRAP

Another trap we fall into, as our society grows, is the trap of large corporations and establishments. In order to focus our energies in a powerful and satisfying way, we must feel confident, certain, and convinced of the righteousness of our actions. However, this can lead to extreme rigidity in thinking in order to maintain a sense of security. There is a tendency to become entrapped within the complex establishments we initially constructed as building blocks on the way to

117

new levels of organized growth, but which have, instead, become ossified into barriers to further growth.

Just as a lobster must be willing to periodically shed its shell in order to grow, even if it means a period of terrible vulnerability until the new becomes solidified, we should be willing to periodically look at all our beliefs and promises from a new perspective. However, the left brain of humans finds security in holding tightly to its own "facts" and "truths" like barnacles to the hull of a ship, attacking all progressive ideas as "heresy," "unconventional," or, "unorthodox." The intellect's security is predicated upon maintaining its beliefs. This is the reason for the progressive rigidity of all social institutions and the power behind ritualistic practices.

Sigmund Freud stated before his death that his own Psychoanalytic Institute had become so rigid that he would not be allowed to remain a member if his name were not Freud. Part of the rigidity which is so common in our institutionalized establishments comes from the mistaken belief that any flexibility or wavering conviction on the part of the people in power will result in a weakening of their person power. Additionally, there is the fear that the acceptance of any new ideas from outside the establishment will empower others who are not part of the establishment.

Rigidity is the main reason for the eventual crumbling of all established institutions. Rigidity in the fixed attitudes and ways of doing things prevents them from keeping up with the changing needs of the times. Sometimes, the power base is so broad and so engraved in the social structure that the restructuring is painfully prolonged. We can see this happening with the educational and medical systems in our country, today.

THE WELFARE TRAP

We must recognize the fact that we all do need to find a sense of significance and fulfillment through some type of performance or activity that makes a contribution to others, as well as to ourselves.

Of all the traps the population of a growing society can fall into, and by far the most deadly, is the trap born of a lack of opportunity for performance, especially within the context of a materialistic society. A healthy society fills the needs of its citizens, protects them from harm, and provides ample opportunities for attaining a sense of significance through the expression of talent and satisfying roles within the structure. For anyone, the ability to obtain satisfying and remunerative work is a primary determinant for a personal sense of significance.

In a democracy, significance is largely dependent upon personal performance. The challenge for personal growth, achievement, status, and security are all placed upon one's own talents and motivation. Devotion is to self first, and to the organization, second. This can result in considerable growth and considerable selfishness as well. Also, as the social structure becomes more complex, more competitive, and more technological, increasingly large segments of the population fall into the category of the inept, those who represent a drain, rather than a resource to the society. Civilizations, as they grow more complex, create increasingly more demands upon its citizens to find a place, and to make a contribution, in order to remain a participant in the sharing of its productivity. A study of history will suggest that the survival of every great civilization was largely dependent upon its ability to care for the growing population of those citizens relegated to the category of inept. The core structure of a civilization depends upon its willingness and its capacity to meet the needs and to integrate within its structure the various groups unable to compete within the structure without special assistance by the structure. While we all have different capabilities and talents, the opportunity for the expression of those talents is not equally available to all. The dissatisfaction of the unemployed festers as a sickness at

119

the core. As the gap widens between the privileged and the deprived, a tolerance breakdown occurs which eventually leads to civil violence.

Giving money and food stamps is not the answer. The more you help, the more you encourage helplessness. Enabling only perpetuates weakness, and postpones the collapse of an unworkable situation. Instead, there must be a fundamental change in the conditions which now foster a feeling of victimization, a pattern of servitude, and a sense of alienation.

Everyone has a need for a special place or role in the social order:

- *A place to rule:* a place where they have a sense of personal power.

- *A place to serve:* an area in which they can make a personal contribution.

In later life, senior citizens who have reached the retirement they worked so long to attain, complain of a loss of identity and sense of significance in our society.

Psychiatrist, Mary Bishop, in her '70's and semi-retired since 1976, comments on the loss of self-worth in both the younger and the older retirees. "People tend to wrap their careers around them, flouting their positions like splendid clothes. They felt vital, needed, and competent in their careers. People sought them out for advice. They got paid for what they did. They had a certain amount of power over others and over their lives. Then, they retired and fell off the significance meter."

Humans, like animals that are maintained in an untenable environment, have the capacity to surrender the life force and die when their life becomes meaningless. The sad part is that in reality, our senior citizens are in a position to understand a whole new meaning to life based upon spiritual values, but most cannot rise above their limited identity with their former work role which, when lost, all too often leaves them with little justification for their existence.

CHAPTER 18(P)

MANAGEMENT OF JUVENILE DELINQUENTS

A reprimand is a mild form of attack, which stirs the survival instinct into resentment. Any approach to establish dominance by intimidating the survival instinct of another person must progressively increase the level of punishment and threats in order to maintain control over the rising level of anger, which this practice incites. Dominance, by force, is always at risk for seemingly unpredictable violence, whether it be by man or by dog.

If our prison system is to have any therapeutic value other than punishment as a deterrent to crime, it must adopt structured programs which shift the attitudes of inmates away from seeking a sense of significance through rebellion and violence, to a new direction which gains self-esteem through mastery. We can only end violence through empowerment, not punishment. However, we do not want to make the mistake of reinforcing a performance trap which is motivated only by achievement. Rather, praise must be directed toward attitude, the willingness to cooperate, the desire to please, and the acceptance of the other person's position of authority without provocation or challenge. This must be, as much as possible, a free will decision if it is to earn legitimate praise. This requires that optional choices, such as "No," are subject to minimal, unemotional consequences, and never to physical punishment nor humiliation. This sounds simplistic, but does it work in practice? I had an impressive first-hand opportunity to observe the praise-versus-reprimand philosophy applied to a group of adolescents who were incarcerated in the California Youth Authority and who were prescreened for an Intensive Treatment Program because of the severity of their social and emotional problems. Nearly all were charged with multiple violations including arson, rape, armed robbery, assault, and murder. Additionally, many were labeled as "incorrigible," at school, at home, in the juvenile halls, and in the group homes where they were previously placed.

121

All psychiatrists receive extensive training in uncovering the root causes of depressed feelings and low self-esteem. We learn how to offer ourselves for the healing experience as a caring, objective listener, and one who allows and accepts the gradual verbal release of emotional tension and who patiently examines very personal trauma in a safe setting. But relatively few psychiatrists receive extensive training in handling violent, rebellious, and out of control behavior in which all of the pent-up frustrations, rage, and self-hate is "acted-out," instead of just talked about. In the short term, such an individual is usually hospitalized and heavily medicated until all the stirred-up biological processes come to rest and rational thinking is once again restored. Then, ideally, the patient will continue with follow-up out-patient therapy to learn how to cope with his feelings by communicating them verbally and by finding more acceptable outlets to prevent their future build-up.

But what about the thousands of teenagers and young adults who are unwilling to or who are unable to communicate their feelings and, instead, have chosen violence as a way of life? My decision to accept a position as psychiatrist in an Intensive Treatment program for disturbed adolescents within the California Youth Authority proved to be an invaluable learning experience for me. I had just completed ten years as Medical Director of a large, multipurpose center for handicapped children and adults in Contra Costa County. In this setting, the love and attention given to these children had of itself, a high therapeutic value. I left convinced from this experience that love, or the lack of it, can dramatically affect a child's I.Q.

But love was definitely not enough when it came to juvenile criminals incarcerated for a variety of violent crimes including assault, rape, armed robbery, and even murder. They had all closed themselves off long ago to the pain of not being loved, and were not ready to put any value or trust again, upon any overtures of love or caring. Additionally, they were filled with self-hate which imposed an impassable barrier to the acceptance of love. The majority came from chaotic, dysfunctional, and abusive homes where language was rarely used for rational communication. The spoken word was used primarily to coerce, intimidate, seduce, control, or to otherwise evoke terror and submission.

Most of the wards felt empty emotionally and saw life as an endless series of problems without solutions. They did not have much hope of changing themselves or bettering their condition. Their underlying anger was so intense that it blocked verbalization of their thoughts. Their feelings and needs had never been integrated into a rational self-dialogue. Instead, they preoccupied themselves with "payback" and revenge as a self-healing process, *i.e.*, as a way of maintaining some sense of significance.

These youths had been deprived of the basic essentials of early training and discipline and consequently had never developed a disciplined mind and had no respect for authority. The question most people might have is, "Is it too late?" In fact, there is some pressure from the general population to extend prison terms and inflict stronger punishments as the only realistic way to protect society at this point. In a real sense, the youthful criminals were much like unsocialized animals and any discipline, to be effective, had to start at the most elementary level, as if we were dealing with children below the age of three or four years. We were able to do this because we had the resources in this setting to physically enforce our limits, similar to that which parents have with young children. Generally, the fewer in number and the more simple the means of enforcement, the more effective. We utilized primarily two modes for compliance: room restriction and temporary soft restraints. Both the imposition and the length of time of these controls were directly related to the ward's behavior. And as with children, coercion, infliction of pain, threats, and reprimand would lead only to rebellion and power struggles. While catering, bribery, and leniency would lead to disrespect and constant limit testing.

Fortunately, the administrator of the Intensive Treatment Unit, Dewey Willis, was a man of considerable experience and had a caring heart for these wards. He set up a highly structured program which implemented, step-by-step, the basic principles of behavioral management:

Behavioral Management Principles

1. Establish yourself in the position of authority.
2. Be consistent.
3. Use praise rather than punishment or blame.

It was crucial to immediately establish our position of authority. There was no question that we were in a position of control in the jailhouse setting, however, the way in which that control was exercised had everything to do with outcome. Basic rules and limits were clearly set and communicated, not only by the staff, but by other wards who had earned leadership positions in the program. This basic orientation was helpful in reducing the fear that comes with feeling helpless in a controlling situation. Expectedly, there would follow a period of days to weeks of aggressive attempts by the new ward to challenge our authority by defying and testing each of the limits. This included a range of behaviors such as profanity, verbal threats, refusal to follow schedules, banging the walls of their room, cracking the look-in window to their room, destroying property, setting fire to their bed, making suicidal gestures and, less often, actually assaulting or attempting to assault other wards and staff. The most destructive behaviors were kept at a minimum through constant staff surveillance and by safe-proofing the environment so that no valuable property or equipment was left exposed to theft or damage. Each behavior was met with a consistent, predictable, unemotional response.

"Unemotional" is the key word here. An emotional charge put upon any communication in a situation of supervision, or from any position of power, has the effect of transforming a correction into a reprimand. A correction is a reminder or a gentle prompting to keep someone on a prescribed course, while a reprimand is an expression of displeasure at willful disobedience. At best, it implies stupidity or ignorance and promotes a sense of guilt, defensiveness, and inferiority. All too often parents with their children, teachers with their students, and bosses with their employees enforce their authority with a tone of reprimand. This may temporarily appear to succeed in promoting servitude responses, however, and especially in the absence of prior positive bonding, it prompts inner resentment or an aggressive counter-response and, in any case, closes off open communication. Any tone of reprimand on the part of the youth counselor, while in the process of reaffirming a limit, would be misinterpreted as degrading or punitive and would trigger the counter-aggressive and survival instincts which these youngsters had learned to maintain at a high state of reactivity. Moreover, once these wards saw that they had the ability to trigger an emotional reaction of any sort (which is called in the jailhouse vernacular, "getting hooked"), they knew how to escalate it into a heavy game of counter-manipulation and an energy-draining power struggle. The ward would declare a "win" if he succeeded in upsetting the counselor or, even better, prompting him to over-react inappropriately so as to set himself up for a disciplinary review by the Administrator.

So long as the defined limits remained unemotionally inflexible, the resistance against them diminished. But, the slightest inconsistency by the staff could lead to endless hassling by the wards, *i.e.*, "I was only five minutes late," or, "I couldn't get up for breakfast because I couldn't get to sleep last night," or, "I whacked him because he wouldn't get out of my face!" "I'm wearing these pants cause my regulation pants don't fit me," etc., etc. On the other hand, no one hassles with the law of gravity, which is both unforgiving and very dependable.

Once the wards accepted the futility of resistance, they began to noticeably relax. It was as if they recognized the fact that the limits worked both ways. The presence of a strong authority in control was now protecting them from abuse and attack. In this setting, they no longer needed to keep their survival mechanisms on a high state of alert, as they did on the streets from which they came. Conforming willingly actually became a way of letting go of a heavy load of internal instability and emotional conflict. This transition occurred, often surprisingly smoothly because there was no power struggle, hence, no sense of defeat or humiliation. On the contrary, for the first time in his life the ward was able to experience a sense of security in knowing that we was in total control of the specific responses he received from the staff. Until now, these youngsters had no idea how their actions affected others. They saw the behavior of others as being totally inner directed, not related to their own behavior, and something beyond their control. Now, they were beginning to develop an "observing ego," which is the ability to stand back and watch the interaction from both sides. They could now substitute the sense of power they felt in "hooking," the other person, for the power of eliciting favorable responses. This predictable action-response pattern with their counselor soon began to establish a security bond to him, and with it, a bond of respect. Now, each compliance had more and more an element of willingness to it.

The slightest willingness to comply was then rewarded with praise. Note that it was the willingness, not the performance, that was praised. We were reinforcing and conditioning an *attitude* that could slowly develop into a stronger, positive bond. The willing attitude was also rewarded with increasing privileges such as having a radio in their room, being allowed to stay up late to watch television in the recreation room, etc.

The program was structured so that the ward could move up four levels of increasing privileges, responsibility, and leadership as he earned them. Rising through these levels depended upon the willingness to maintain a disciplined mind in school performance, personal hygiene, work assignments, therapy groups, and recreational activities. With this came the ability to be a role model to the other wards. These opportunities for mastery and recognition had a powerful, inbuilt, self-motivating force because of their associated positive enhancement to self-concept. Also, whenever an opportunity is made available to move up the pecking order in any structured system, this significantly reduces anger and the sense of helplessness. Aggressive energy can now be channeled into self-improvement.

The average stay in the program was one year. It was truly amazing to see the changes some of the wards made during this time, not only in personal self-care and relationship behaviors, but also in supporting and counseling the newer wards. I remember fondly one particular young man, Steven, who was taken from his parents at an early age because of severe abuse, and raised in foster homes where he continued to experience various forms of physical and emotional abuse. He was almost illiterate and had never learned to articulate his needs and his feelings. Anger was the only emotion he identified with. He escaped from his inner void and feelings of fear by finding outside targets for his hate. The only way in which he knew how to find any sense of significance was to create chaos in his environment, and to thus become the focus of major upset and concern by the caretakers and the authority figures who had assumed responsibility for him. His behavior was much like that of a wild, caged animal when he first came to the unit. He had never known of any way to earn praise for his behavior. But once given the opportunity, he responded to praise like a plant that turns its leaves to the sun. His transformation into a leader, over the year he was on the Wintu Lodge, is a real tribute to the praise vs. reprimand approach. This structured setting demonstrated the indisputable fact that praise is always a much stronger motivating factor than reprimand, and that behavior is strongly related to environmental conditioning.

I wish I could conclude a more positive ending to this story. However, after discharge, statistical follow-ups indicated that the majority of even the most improved wards, once they returned to their unstructured and dehumanizing home environments, reverted to their previous delinquent behaviors. Environmental conditioning, without continuous support, is difficult, if not impossible, for most individuals to overcome.

Product of Alpha Dog Dominant Training

Reprogrammed with Mutual Respect

GRAPH #1

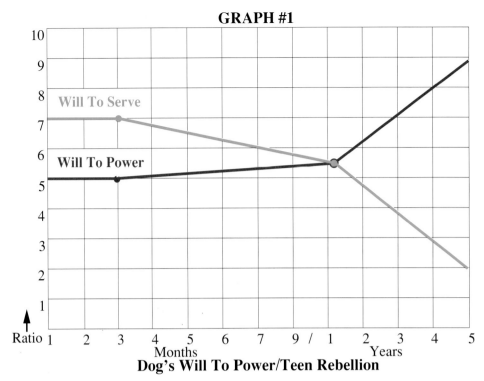

Will To Serve

Will To Power

Ratio

Months

Years

Dog's Will To Power/Teen Rebellion

GRAPH #2

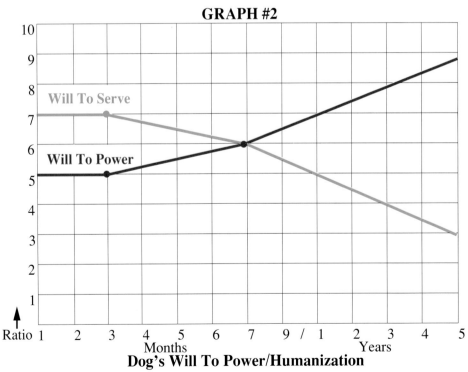

Will To Serve

Will To Power

Ratio

Months

Years

Dog's Will To Power/Humanization

130

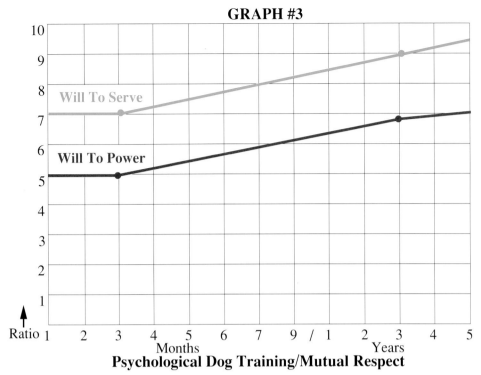

GRAPH #3

Will To Serve

Will To Power

Ratio

Months | Years

Psychological Dog Training/Mutual Respect

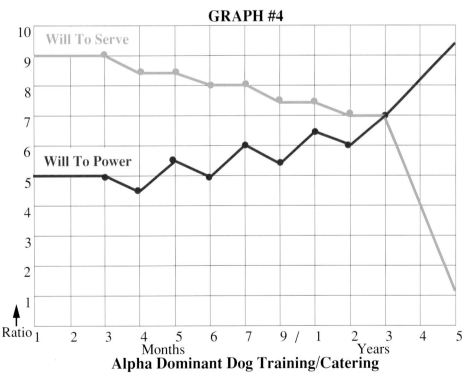

GRAPH #4

Will To Serve

Will To Power

Ratio

Months | Years

Alpha Dominant Dog Training/Catering

Disciplined Mind

Fear Conditioning

Emotional Conditioning

Adrenal
Stimulation

Excitement

Flight

Hyperactivity

Fight

COMPARISON OF THE BRAIN OF
MAN AND DOG

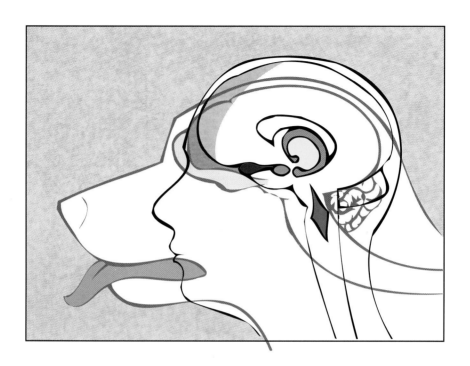

The Five Centers Regulating Aggression and Violence in Man and Dog

A. *Reticular Activating System* (blue)
B. *Amygdala* (green)
C. *Limbic System* (orange)
D. *Hypothalamus/Thalmus* (yellow)
E. *Outer Cortex (frontal lobes)*
     Man's (light gray)
     Dog's (dark gray)
Man Outline (black)
Man Olfactory Bulb (purple)
Dog Outline and Olfactory Bulb (brown)

Stress-Rest Pattern
In The Animal Kingdom

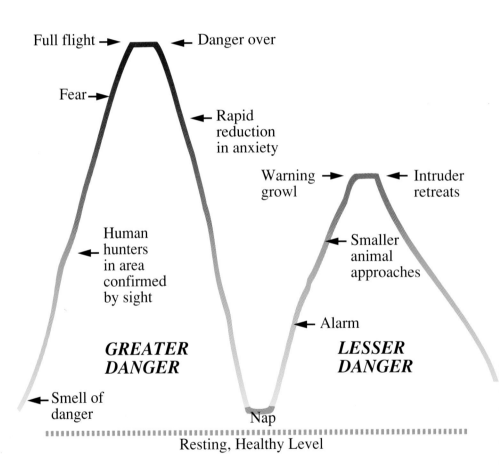

Full flight → ← Danger over

Fear →

← Rapid reduction in anxiety

Warning → ← Intruder
growl retreats

← Human hunters in area confirmed by sight

← Smaller animal approaches

← Alarm

GREATER DANGER

LESSER DANGER

← Smell of danger

Nap

Resting, Healthy Level

Example Of Stress-No Rest Pattern In Humans

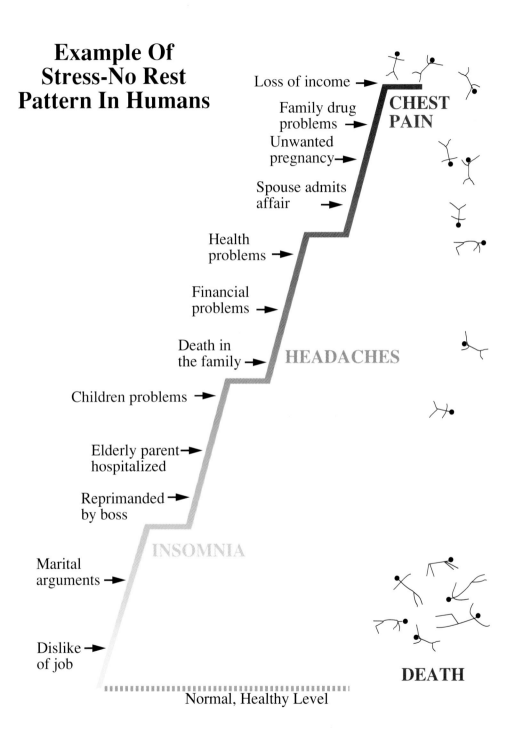

Loss of income →

CHEST PAIN

Family drug problems →

Unwanted pregnancy →

Spouse admits affair →

Health problems →

Financial problems →

Death in the family →

HEADACHES

Children problems →

Elderly parent → hospitalized

Reprimanded → by boss

INSOMNIA

Marital arguments →

Dislike → of job

DEATH

Normal, Healthy Level

"Going Off"
Anger-To-Violence Syndrome

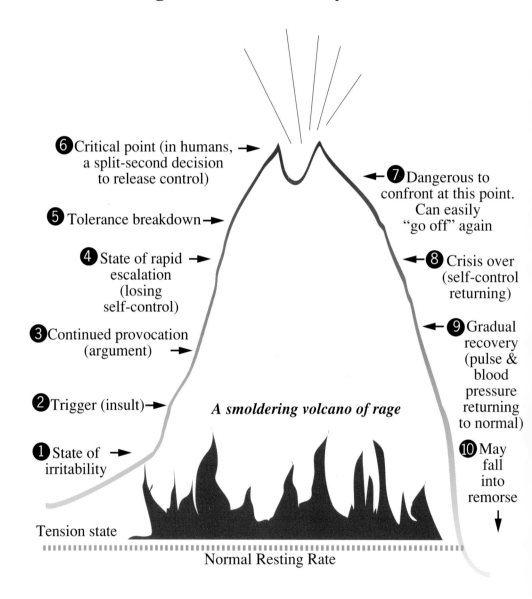

6 Critical point (in humans, a split-second decision to release control)

5 Tolerance breakdown

4 State of rapid escalation (losing self-control)

3 Continued provocation (argument)

2 Trigger (insult)

1 State of irritability

A smoldering volcano of rage

7 Dangerous to confront at this point. Can easily "go off" again

8 Crisis over (self-control returning)

9 Gradual recovery (pulse & blood pressure returning to normal)

10 May fall into remorse

Tension state

Normal Resting Rate

CHAPTER 19(M)

ALPHA DOMINANT TRAINING - Dog/Abuse

The "Back to Nature" movement applying the dominant methods of the Wolf pack leader swept the country in record time. The main reason I believe it was so readily adopted is that our culture constantly seeks ways to make things more efficient to save time. This certainly has its place; yet, when it comes to training a dog or teaching a student, time is a factor. When you speed up beyond the individual's ability to absorb and retain, the mind gets flustered and the brain seems to short circuit.

When force/pressure is used, a rebellious resistance to the applicator is triggered and comes into play. Now a problem exists where there may not have been one and the student becomes stubborn and hard-headed and is difficult to teach. Perhaps the teacher/trainer becomes angry and flustered. Thus, one of the most important teaching principles — "mutual respect" — is lost. The whole structure bonding teacher to student (be it human or animal) starts to crumble.

A rebellious behavior forms within the being who is supposed to be learning from the teacher/trainer. The frustration builds until it becomes explosive, sometimes to the level of life or death survival. This is exactly what happens when dominant training methods are used on a dog that has a high will-to-power/survival. The dog will not accept this mental/emotional/physical abuse. This requires the owner or dog trainer to apply more physical force until the dog surrenders his will to the trainer. Sometimes it takes two people to make the dog submit.

Some owners/trainers are surprised when even a sweet young puppy fights back when suddenly threatened and abused with the Alpha Dog roll over — such was the case of a Shar Pei I had to eventually reprogram. John, a first-time dog owner, purchased a dog training book and followed the author/trainer's advice to the letter. The first thing it said was to establish dominance over your puppy by becoming the Alpha Dog leader of the pack. Following the instructions, John suddenly picked up Sid (his puppy) and threw him onto his back in the Alpha Dog rollover position. As he was about to go into phase two — stare Sid in the eyes while holding him by the throat with both hands — John was totally unprepared for what happened next. Sid exploded like a one-ton bomb and before John could even understand or respond, Sid had bitten him twice, once on the hand and the second time on the forearm. Confused, John backed off while Sid bared his teeth. I believe that if John *had not gone back* to this "highly recommended" book he would have been able to re-evaluate the whole scenario and, with good old fashioned, think-it-through common sense, would have realized that Sid was not the type of dog described by the book's author. A whole different approach could have been substituted. Unfortunately, this did not happen.

John picked up Sid and scruff-shook him. When Sid tried to retaliate and bite, John managed this time to avoid it by throwing Sid down on the floor. John figured his pup was not getting his leadership message because he was too young. Wanting no more biting incidents, John decided he needed some professional instruction offered by a local dog obedience school at the humane society once a week. The price was right and the meetings were scheduled for evenings. The flyer read, "We train with love and positive methods." It looked like a green light and John signed up for the class. Within 5 minutes, the light changed from green to yellow when the instructor informed the class, "You need to be your dog's Alpha Leader," as owners were marching side-by-side. One dog bumped into Sid and Sid growled at him. Before John could react, the instructor, saying, "You're not firm enough with your dog," yanked the leash out of John's hands and started jerking Sid as hard as she could while screaming at the dog, "No! No! No!" Sid's growling increased each time the instructor gave Sid a jerk. Refusing to submit to this abuse, Sid lunged at her and, before John could open his mouth, Sid was hanging off the ground by his neck. At this point John saw red and grabbed the leash away from the woman. She reprimanded him for being too *weak*. Needless to say, that was the first and last day in class for John and Sid.

After this experience, Sid became even more aggressive and would growl when his owner tried to put him on the leash to take him for a walk. After a few months with no change in Sid's aggressiveness, he sought the help of a professional dog trainer to evaluate Sid. The trainer informed John that he was not firm enough in the early training so that Sid did not accept him as the leader. The trainer convinced John that getting really tough was the answer.

With Sid securely tied on a short chain to a tree in the backyard, the trainer extended his hand towards Sid and agitated him. As soon as Sid lunged for the trainer he was whacked with a red rubber hose across the muzzle (See the Chapter on Power Struggle, Red Rubber Hose). Sid was shocked and backed off. The next few times that the trainer tried to agitate Sid into lunging or even growling Sid just stood there with his tail between his legs. This seemingly total submission of Sid's aggressive behavior appeared to prove the trainers point of "Get Tough." Sid remained a meek dog for about a week. Then one day he growled as John went to snap on the leash. The next day an appointment was made for a reinforcement of the "Get Tough," "Be Top Dog." Again Sid was chained to the tree and once again the trainer proceeded to teach Sid a lesson. But this time Sid was more aggressive and would not back down. Sid fought back every time he was 'rubber-hosed'. After about 15 to 20 minutes the trainer stopped and advised John that because his dog should really respond to John it would be best if he put Sid through his paces a couple of times each day for a couple of weeks. A good idea would be to get a pair of metal mesh, reinforced gloves to prevent Sid from biting through them, because it would be necessary for John to put his hand right into Sid's face. Also to get a PVC (hard plastic) pipe to be more "effective." John was not too sure if he was capable of doing that so the trainer offered to come back and demonstrate how it should be done.

After three private training sessions the trainer had accomplished his goal. Sid would back off and only growl when he was agitated. Sid was hit so many times that his scalp began bleeding and required veterinarian treatment. After John explained the cause of Sid's bleeding, the veterinarian wanted to file charges of animal cruelty against the trainer. Unfortunately, the trainer disappeared into the night and moved to another city.

Sid would try to bite John's hand every time it was necessary to snap on his leash for his outside toilet duty. John had to leave the leash on even in the house in order not to trigger Sid's memory of his brutalization.

When I first met Sid for testing he was on a 10-foot line. It took 10 days of reprogramming to establish enough trust so that I could put my hand close to his head. After 4 weeks I was able to overcome his head shyness. Once again he permitted the leash to be snapped on and off when I took him out of his kennel run. His innate willingness to work and please, conditioned with respect and trust, overruled his survival aggressiveness.

After 9 weeks and 6 private one-on-one sessions, John and Boy (Sid's new name), were friends and bonded for the first time.

I have been asked to reprogram many dogs that never bonded and would even bite their owners — all because they were dominant trained with the Alpha Dog roll-over, pin-them-down and hold-them-to-the-ground technique. Even puppies can remember these negative/disrespectful techniques and will not respect or trust their owners. Thus, the need to growl or bite which is the basic survival instinct.

I have found the following methods to be the cause of 85% of the behavioral problems in dogs that I have worked with:

DOMINANT TRAINING

1. *THE HARD JERK*

In this system the dog owner is instructed to get an extra firm grip on the leash and to pivot from the waist to ensure extra leverage to jerk the dog firmly when he makes a mistake. If the dog snarls and snaps, a repetition with an even harder jerk accompanied by a loud *"NO"* is recommended. If the dog attempts to bite again, the final suggestion is to seek the help of a professional trainer.

My comment: How absurd that a professional gives advice to the dog owner knowingly setting him up for a possible bite by his dog;

then relieves himself from the responsibility of the negative consequences of his teaching method by recommending the help of a professional. (Who?)

A professional should not give any advice to a dog owner which makes a dog more aggressive.

2. *ALPHA-DOG METHOD* (Lift-Up/Roll-Over/Stare Method)

This training technique was derived from the behavior of wolves and is an incorrect interpretation of the method of the pack leader in maintaining the ranking order.

The enhanced "human" version consists of lifting up the dog by the scruff of his neck and throwing him on his back to the ground, holding him down and staring into his eyes.

This so-called alpha-wolf or alpha-dog method is an entirely imperfect copy of the genuine interaction of wild canines and even domestic dogs. It completely overlooks the fact that every pack member knows his position within the group, and a weaker animal usually assumes a submissive posture "voluntarily," and the dominant one does not need to throw him on his back. Even in a ritualized dominance fight the loser gives in by submission without a further contest of wills.

When a dog owner (who is in no way respected by his dog as the leader) throws the pet on his back forcing him into a submissive position, fear and rebellion can be created in the animal. Unfortunately, man applies canine customs imperfectly and perverts them to enforce his leadership over his dog with the intention of conditioning and accustoming the dog to the human environment.

This method, used for establishing a system of rank and order between man and dog, is doomed to fail not only because it is wrongly applied, but also because the days of the wolf pack leader are numbered from the beginning. His position is only temporary and is jeopardized as soon as he drops his guard. An alpha dog remains in his leader position only as long as he is physically strong and mentally alert enough to cope with his challenging subordinates. This guarantees that only the strongest and fittest is in the power position in order to insure the survival of the pack.

The behavior of canine superiors and inferiors is governed by set rules originating from their hereditary patterns. In other words, there is a certain fixed and binding behavior associated with the ranking order. We human beings, accustomed to double standards and making compromises, are not able to adhere to those strict canine rules. The dog will immediately notice our failure every time.

The most vulnerable position, which a dog assumes in response to a dominating adversary, is to "voluntarily" get down on his back and present his unprotected belly. He can be forced to do this only as long as he feels weaker than his rival. *He no longer will accept this* when he feels stronger than his adversary. The dog will use any opportunity to retaliate against his opponent and challenge him. This is one of the main reasons why many dog trainers, who teach puppy socialization classes, will not accept any dogs over six months old.

A dog, trained and made forcefully obedient by a human being with the alpha-dog method, feels completely insecure and will attempt to subordinate his owner. From the dog's point of view the human has no real authority. The dog will promote himself to the leader rank as soon as he reaches maturity and feels strong enough. The dog can then cast off his obedience to his owner's commands learned as a puppy. The dog conditioned with this method revolts with unprovoked assaults on other animals, children, adults and eventually his owner. He proves his new position as top dog.

When you engage in a battle of the wills, which is the essence of the alpha-wolf/alpha-dog and other forceful methods, the stronger individual aggressively dominates the weaker one. The dog has the best possible tools to eventually reach this goal — his teeth. An emotionally weaker dog trained with the alpha-dog method becomes more and more intimidated. He will exhibit increasing shyness and fearfulness. His growing and overwhelming insecurity will result in the slightest incident triggering his self-preservation instinct, ending with a bite. It's a vicious cycle. As many examples prove, there is no doubt that this is a very dangerous method, especially with a full-grown, large dog.

Some authors/trainers mention the possible dangers of using the alpha-dog method on highly aggressive, large and mature dogs, and recommend instead employing the services of a professional to "dominate" the rebellious pet. However, this method is not even "foolproof" when practiced by a trainer. During one of my seminars on psychological dog training, a student told in class about a demonstration of the alpha-dog roll which she had witnessed.

A well-known and successful local trainer attempted to demonstrate a roll-over in a group-training class with an aggressive, three-year-old Akita. To ensure the safety of the trainer, the dog was muzzled and had a cord tied around his face and head. During the "domination" struggle the tie around the dog's jaws came loose, the muzzle came off, and the trainer ended up with 39 stitches on his face. Because of this incident, the Akita was condemned as unsalvageable, and the owners, who loved this dog very much, had to make the emotionally difficult decision to have the dog destroyed.

One author tells the reader to surprise his dog and suddenly shove the dog into the alpha-dog roll-over with vigor — I wonder how many dog owners have been bitten when they attempted this on their own mature dog? I have tested many dogs who bit their owners when they were only 12 weeks old.

3. *THE SCRUFF SHAKE*
This method says to: Grasp your dog with both hands on his neck scruff and stare into his eyes. Then violently shake him from side to side scolding him in a low, loud tone with, "No." Even more effective is lifting your dog up in the air while staring directly into his eyes, shouting, and shaking him, and then abruptly dropping him to the ground.

This method was "created" by observing the mother dog lifting up her immature pups with her mouth and slightly shaking them when they misbehaved. Obviously, it has not been considered that she does this only to the helpless, very young pups. When they are older, she keeps them in line just with an oral reprimand.

Be thankful that the instructions do not advise you to use this method to the full extent, by lifting up the dog with your teeth instead of your hands.

4. *THE UPPERCUT*

Another method instructs you to: Teach your dog discipline by hitting him under the chin. Be sure to hit the pet hard enough to get at least a yelp. Otherwise it will not be sufficient.

What does a yelp from your dog mean? There can be no doubt that this is an expression of pain and fear.

Another trainer/author wanted to top-dog this concept by instructing the reader (and her group obedience class) to not swing at your dog and hit him on the side of his face as you may break his lower jaw. The proper thing to do when Fido snaps or even growls is to make a closed fist and hit him underneath hard enough to cause his head to snap back. But she warns the reader not to break the dog's neck — be humane. What is so shocking is that these instructions of hitting the puppy with a closed fist have been published by a prominant Humane Society and is distributed throughout the U.S. to other Humane Societies and animal shelters.

I will never accept (or understand) how this type of thinking can be considered humane.

5. *THE STRINGING UP AND HANGING*

Another method being used and taught by trainers, especially in group obedience classes, is to string the dog up. This is used when a dog misbehaves or is disobedient, and when the other methods of heavy jerking, hitting under the chin, and yelling do not lead to the desired results.

Dog owners are instructed to hold the chain short, lift the dog off the ground and hang him there until he is gasping for breath. They are then supposed to drop the dog to the floor before he suffocates.

For highly aggressive dogs, one inhumane trainer even recommends pounding the obstinate pet in midair, striking him on the muzzle with a wood-reinforced rubber hose.

6. *RUBBER HOSE/PLASTIC P.V.C. PIPE/WOODEN DOWEL*

The object in dominant training is to make the dog submit to a stronger force if the dog fights back. The innocent dog owner is informed that this behavior shows the dog trying to be top dog. Then force concept techniques are increased to higher and higher pain inducing levels. If that does not work, one noted author/trainer advises the owner to put a wooden dowel inside of the rubber hose or P.V.C. pipe to be more effective. The bottom line is you either break the dog's spirit into submission or you break open his head or have him destroyed because of his survival, want-to-live instinct. How tragically sad!

CHAPTER 20(P)

DOMINANCE TRAINING

A misconception over establishing dominance and obtaining obedient behavior has resulted in a serious misapplication into the training methods of dogs of what supposedly happens in nature. The result has been a significant increase in violent behavior by household pets, which has important implications in terms of human behavior, as well.

First, dominance is established by a variety of visual or behavioral cues which do not involve the brutalization of other pack members. Only in special situations where dominance is challenged does it involve a physical contest. Secondly, establishing dominance is not directly related to establishing responsibility or authority within the social system. For example, a bully in the school yard may establish dominance by his threatening demeanor, but not necessarily obedience, and certainly not loyalty. Obedience from dogs and from children is dependent upon establishing a devotional bond based upon mutual trust and respect. Dominance based upon intimidation may obtain momentary subservient compliance, but eventually anger will overcome fear and then rebellion or violence may be the result.

Additionally, currently accepted dominance training methods in dogs can result in permanent injury to the brain and to the spinal cord at its juncture in the neck where it enters the skull. Vigorously shaking the head back and forth can result in shearing injuries and contusions to the soft structures of the brain. A common injury is the "contre coupe" type injury where injury to the occipital lobes in the back of the head results from a sharp blow to the forehead, because of a whiplash effect. At least one case has been reported of a child becoming permanently blind as the result of her head being shaken roughly back and forth by a babysitter. Contusions, shearing, and microhemmorhages within the brain can occur from the methods of training promoted by the Alpha-Dominant advocates. Children who witness their parents administering this harsh and unloving training

147

method upon their young puppy can be expected to believe that this is the way in which they should also establish their own importance over younger siblings and susceptible children in the playground. Later, they might creatively improvise upon this art of ruthless intimidation and apply it emotionally to the corporate world.

Unconditional obedience is expected and demanded in a number of healthy relationship dyads including those of field commander-soldier, king-countryman, conductor-pianist, maestro-student, spiritual leader-disciple, coach-player, and, ideally, parent-child. This is a highly efficient model for teaching, ruling, or waging war, because there is no friction, no energy-wasting power struggles, and relatively little need for dealing with disobedience because the dominant position of the leader is unquestioned.

But all this changes dramatically when there is contempt or disrespect on either side of the equation, regardless of the cause or the justification. (We see this in many of our inner city public schools.) Now, there is inner questioning, passive or open resistance to orders, and the build-up of resentment which requires significant policing to discourage rebellion. The use of physical punishment always denotes the failure of discipline. And, discipline only fails when there is a lack of mutual respect and trust.

Punishment, or the threat of punishment, involving pain and/or prolonged physical confinement is still believed to be an effective deterrent to rebellious behavior, as well as a way to insure future compliance. Instead, it results in promoting fear, resentment, and a sense of injustice which may actually compel a repetition of the forbidden behavior. It significantly severs whatever bond there may have existed between the two parties, whether it be state and criminal or parent and child. Communication thereafter deteriorates to mechanical and subservient responses, masking simmering rage and the wish for revenge. This increases the need for vigilance, surveillance, and policing to insure obedience.

Dictatorships that are imposed upon the people of a territory or state often attempt to attain unconditional obedience by inflicting sufficiently severe and cruel punishments upon every person evidencing any attitude of rebellion, in the mistaken belief that the will of the people will be broken as they come to realize that all resistance is useless. But, this can never be effective for long with a population that has tasted freedom, or has knowledge of other countries which live more happily under a model of benign leadership. Unfortunately, some parents run their family like a dictatorship not realizing that, with a bond of love and devotion, oppression and punishment is entirely unnecessary, and when resorted to by an insecure parent, represents a cruel misuse of power, an act of violence.

Democracies, on the other hand, are not dependent upon unconditional obedience to a leader. Political figures are frequently criticized, second-guessed, and assailed by opponents and various advocate groups. The acceptance of expressions of protest through marches, free speech, letters to the editor, public forums, etc., helps to temper aggression by offering an outlet for frustration. The system works so long as it is sustained by a respect for the system. The leader becomes less important than the system. When people lose faith in the system, they oppose it in ways that promote aggression or disobedience of its laws. A democracy is not structured to control a dissident population. Only a dictatorship can do that. Thus, failed democracies, *i.e.*, democracies that cannot sustain a viable economy or protect its citizens from violence, are vulnerable to the establishment of a dictatorship with the consent of the people.

CHAPTER 21(M)
THERAPY TRAINING

Reprogramming a dog's behavior through therapy training has been the most rewarding activity in my work. It far exceeds training a dog for competition, be it A.K.C. obedience or field and water retrieving trials. I have known the ego-glow of beating the competitors and their dogs many times. Just reflecting on it, I can still feel the adrenal surge and the intensity of awareness heighten, which was my edge when competing. Looking back in time, I now understand and realize why I felt the need to drop out of competitive activity while I was at a peak 29 years ago.

The training of competitive dogs for top performance was based not only on conditioning the uniqueness of man's best friend's willingness to please and work for us (W.T.S.), but also on the stimulation of the adrenal system. This involved a very balanced amount of control, especially in the case of some high-spirited dogs I have trained, one of which was my own dog, the German Shorthair Pointer, Baroness.

Therapy training requires a completely opposite approach. The Will-to-Serve by means of a disciplined mind is primarily conditioned in a calmer non-competitive dog. The essential difference is that the adrenal system is not stimulated but calmed down. The best way I can describe this distinction is to quote a client and friend of mine, Jan Kass, whose overly territorial dog needed reprogramming: "Duffin now seems to be on Zen. He's always so peaceful and does not get triggered by the activity that used to excite him." His disciplined mind had been so much strengthened that his adrenals no longer controlled his behavior.

Reprogramming the Pecking Order

On the other end of the spectrum is the reprogramming of passive dogs with very little self-assertiveness. This mental gymnastics may be compared to what Dr. Maltz illustrates in his book, *Psycho-cybernetics*, regarding the performance of two professional basketball teams that were put through training practice. Team A was given the opportunity to practice and compete with other basketball teams. The only team they could not play with was team B.

For the players of team B, Dr. Maltz designed a training program which was unique at the time. Though team B was to compete with team A after this experiment, the players were not permitted to be on or near a basketball court. Also, they were not allowed to physically practice either individually or as a team. Their practice consisted of merely sitting in a chair and mentally playing on the court against other teams. Though this may have seemed somewhat bizarre to some, their team comradeship came through.

The effect of this psychocybernetic training became obvious when team B met team A to play each other. Their overall playing performance was almost equal. The results must have surprised both the players and those who evaluated and directed this imaging experiment.

Dogs do not have a large frontal lobe for rationalization, thus, are not able to apply psychocybernetic principles. Yet, with some problem dogs it was possible to set up scenarios where the dog experienced a non-physical happening, which was registered by the brain, and the dog was able to recall the experience as if he physically went through it.

The following is such a story that took place in 1968. At that time I was, myself, in the experimental trial/error stages of self-teaching in psychoanalyzing and therapy reprogramming problematic canines.

RALPH

I took Monty, the Bullmastiff, out of his run and, on leash, led him down the row of kenneled dogs. As we neared the last run, a small white dog bounded against the gate, barking at Monty. The big dog regarded him tolerantly. I smiled. Monty could have swallowed the little 10-pound terrier mix in one gulp, had he the inclination to do so.

But I was proud of Ralph's plucky spirit. I'd worked hard to get him to that point, and it was quite a contrast to his former behavior.

He had first entered my kennel twelve weeks before, in the arms of his owner, Mrs. Jensen. Every hair on his body seemed to quiver in fright as the woman explained the reasons for which she had come. "I already had two dogs before I acquired Ralph," she said. "Mutt and Jeff are very outgoing and full of mischief. I had gotten Ralph because I thought they would like another dog to play with."

"How do the other dogs react to Ralph?" I asked. "Well, Mutt and Jeff have always loved to roughhouse with each other. Since Ralph has come into the picture, they team up and pounce on him every chance they get. Ralph is so afraid of them now that he spends most of his time in my bedroom, under the bed. He won't even come out to eat. I have to place his food under the bed for him. I have tried to get him accustomed to the rest of the house and to the other dogs, but as soon as I take him out and let him go, he scurries right back into my bedroom. I've never had a dog that has done that before. I don't know what to do."

Mrs. Jensen had pinpointed the problem. Ralph was much too sensitive to be jostled and bullied by the other two dogs. He was at the bottom of the pecking order and his only refuge was under his owner's bed. I explained this to Mrs. Jensen and advised her to find a home for Ralph with no other dogs for him to compete with.

"Oh, dear," she said frowning. "I didn't want to give him away. I love all three of my dogs. Can't you teach him not to be afraid of the other dogs?"

I thought for a moment. "Well, I could possibly build up his self-image, if that is what you mean. It might take some doing, but it is a feasible alternative to giving him away." "When can he start?" she said without hesitation.

I began Ralph's training with a relaxed, unpressured program to get him accustomed to the newness of his situation. I would walk him around the ring, whistling and talking to him until he finally relaxed. Once we had established a master-dog relationship through basic obedience, Ralph became more secure within himself, and his constant apprehension of being ambushed, eventually faded. Now he was ready for his image-building course.

I pondered how best to go about this next stage. It was going to be a delicate process to be sure. I had to set up a foolproof situation in which Ralph would have the upper hand. I decided to begin by using the ducks that I keep for retriever training. I let them out of their pen and went back to the kennel for Ralph.

The ducks were milling around the yard as we approached. Ralph was reluctant to get near them until he saw that they would waddle away if we came too close. Soon we were chasing them all over the yard. Ralph thought it was great fun to have something run from *him* for a change. Within three days, Ralph was eagerly anticipating our duck chases.

In order to broaden his experience, I set about walking him through our open fields where I train pheasant dogs, hoping to find a sitting jack rabbit to chase. I finally spotted one, laying low in a clump of grass. Ears down, the rabbit was as still as a statue. We crept closer, then suddenly charged. The jack rabbit darted out of its spot and bounded across the field with us in hot pursuit. We were no match for the rabbit's swiftness, of course, but the chase did wonders for Ralph's ego. He barked excitedly at the rapidly disappearing form. Every day thereafter, when our basic obedience sessions were over, Ralph and I would chase all the jack rabbits out of the fields.

I devised a somewhat more elaborate scheme to extend Ralph's confidence around other dogs. I used a Labrador Retriever that I had been training for duck-work. I took the Lab out and gave her a sit-stay command at one end of the training ring. Next, I placed a retrieving bumper behind her back at the opposite end of the training ring. Then I brought Ralph out. When we came within twenty feet of the Lab, Ralph let out a surprised bark. I immediately gave the Lab a hand signal for "back." When the Lab turned and ran back for the bumper, it appeared as though Ralph had chased her off. I reinforced the illusion by trotting after the retreating dog with Ralph running alongside of me. When the Lab picked up the bumper and turned to bring it to me, I had to stop her quickly with a sharp blast on my field whistle so that it wouldn't appear that she was coming after Ralph. She sat holding the bumper and I gave her a *stay* hand signal. Ralph must have felt ten feet tall. As I picked up the "conquering hero" and carried him away from the other dog, he looked back at the Lab and gave a final indignant bark.

After the episode with the Lab, Ralph was starting to feel his muscles. He would boldly investigate other dogs as we walked past their runs, and sometimes even bark at them. Ralph, although friendly and affectionate, was no longer the meek and mild-mannered dog he once had been. I felt a suitable nickname was in order, and decided upon "Tiger."

The transfer sessions with Mrs. Jensen went smoothly. She was extremely pleased with her little dog and she even liked his new name. I asked her to bring Mutt and Jeff along when she came for the last session. Ralph was going to have to confront these two, and I wanted to be on hand when he did. It was going to be Ralph's supreme test, for up to that point, all his "conquests" had been imaginary ones.

Mutt and Jeff were waiting in the car, and after the session was over, we took him out for the confrontation. The two dogs barked and wagged their tails excitedly when they saw good ol' Ralph coming. Life had probably been pretty dull without him. They watched from the rear platform area of the station wagon as I opened the back door and gave Ralph the "kennel" (which means "in") command. He jumped up on the back seat and I closed the door. That was Mutt and Jeff's cue. They came flying over the backrest and landed on Ralph. Mutt pinned him down and quickly grabbed an ear, while Jeff took hold of Ralph's tail and began to tug on it. The two dogs were really getting down to business when Ralph exploded out from under Mutt, bowling him over. Before Mutt could recover, he found himself on his back, with Ralph standing over him growling menacingly. Jeff, startled at the sudden reversal, had let go of Ralph's tail and jumped back over the backrest to "safety." Mutt was too surprised to do anything but submit to Ralph.

I waited a couple of minutes for Ralph to establish, beyond any doubt, who would be number one from now on. Then I stuck my head through the open window. "Okay, Ralph. That will do." He looked up at me and wagged his tail. Mutt seized the opportunity to disengage himself and fly over the backrest to join Jeff.

There was something almost majestic in the way Ralph looked, sitting there with the whole back seat all to himself. I felt sure that he'd never abuse his new-found strength by bullying Mutt and Jeff. But he had made it clear, they wouldn't have Ralph to pick on anymore.

MUTT WAS TOO SUPRISED TO DO ANYTHING BUT
SUBMIT TO RALPH...

CHAPTER 22(P)

THE GENETIC/BIOLOGICAL/INSTINCTIVE
BASIS FOR BEHAVIOR

The patterns of aggression which are innate in every animal, are not automatically linked to hostile emotion or to destructive goals. In fact, these patterns form the basis for play activities, such as chasing, running away, wrestling, etc. These patterns in humans may be refined, with practice, into specialized skills used in sports, such as basketball, football, tennis, and recreational activities, such as dancing.

In carnivorous animals, such as a large cat, aggressive attack patterns against a prey for food purposes is made without warning and with relatively little emotion on the part of the attacker. A different mechanism is involved when the animal's territory is invaded. The animal gives a warning sound, such as a snarl, to alert the intruder that his alarm system is on. If the intruder leaves, the alarm system subsides and the aggressive pattern is avoided.

If the intruder is a larger animal who persists in invasive behavior, then a very different and defensive pattern may be triggered. The cat's body will stiffen up, the hairs on its back will rise, and it will hiss in an attempt to discourage further aggression. Anger and rage reactions are now triggered which overcome fear and which mobilize the body to sustain an attack. Again, this response is designed to discourage aggression or to defend against it, and does not have violence as its aim.

In humans, however, anger and rage is perpetuated by angry thoughts which fester and build up in intensity over time, without any additional stimulation. Whereas in animals, aggressive emotions quickly die down unless they are being continually fed, anger and rage in humans is *always* the result of perceived attack, coupled with a sense of relative helplessness. In animals, anger and rage subside when the immediate threat is removed, but humans will continue to nurse indefinitely, the feelings of humiliation and personal insult, and will fantasize opportunities for revenge long after the event which triggered these feelings, until the urge for violence, given appropriate weapons, becomes irresistible. Thus, a pattern in nature which is limited to defensive purposes in the face of imminent threat becomes, in humans, a justification for unrestrained and premeditated violence.

THE BIOLOGICAL ROOTS OF ANGER

Anger springs from the deepest and most primitive part of the brain. Electrodes placed against the hypothalamus of cats can induce instant rage at the flip of a switch. The cerebral cortex, the reasoning part of the brain, covers and controls these inner primitive centers. Walter Cannon, the famous physiologist from Harvard University, was intrigued by his discovery in the 1930's that the removal of the cerebral hemispheres resulted in an extraordinary exhibition of rage. Similarly, anything that disturbs the regulatory function of the cerebral cortex, i.e., brain damage, drugs, alcohol, malnutrition, and chronic stress, can result in increased irritability, intolerance to stress, frustration, and acts of violence.

Anger blocks thinking and creativity, constricts the flow of blood to the internal organs, holds the heart in a tight grip and, literally, blinds us to the potential for loving communication with others. When a person is in a state of extreme rage, his body is flushed with adrenalin and the rational part of the brain is partially paralyzed. Rage behavior is momentarily under the control of instinctive survival reactions or learned responses from earlier experiences and the modeling examples of adults who experienced rage during childhood.

HOW THE MIND INFLUENCES ANGER

What may appear to an observer as senseless violence, always makes sense to the perpetrator. With rare exceptions, violence is always premeditated and perceived as justifiable behavior. Even when it appears to be the result of sudden provocation, the violent act is always previously rehearsed, over and over, in the mind of the

158

perpetrator awaiting the proper justification for expression. Because of this built-in sense of righteousness, it is extremely rare for a perpetrator of violence to experience any real remorse for the victim, even years later. On the contrary, rehearsing the incident in the mind, later, often reactivates the original feelings of violence and the desire to repeat it. Given the same set of circumstances again, we can predict that the act will be repeated, be it wife beating or murder.

LEARNED HELPLESSNESS AND DEPRESSION

There is still another response to perceived danger which animals exhibit, with parallels for humans. When an animal cannot run from the threat and cannot fight it, another part of its autonomic nervous system, called the parasympathetic nervous system, is activated which may shut down all aggressive responses. In its attempt to minimize the energy of impending attack, or to remain in hiding, an animal assumes a posture of total helplessness by "playing dead." The emotion experienced by the animal in this posture, is depression. Physiologically, the responses associated with depression are those that blur consciousness, numb pain, and decrease the fear of death.

In recent years, the syndrome of "learned helplessness," has been recognized by therapists as a habitual coping mechanism which some people adopt to meet life challenges, and which is a variant of the animal pattern of submission, or depression, in the face of a threat. This is consistent with Freud's early theories of depression which hypothesize that depression is the result of anger turned inward. While a person with a hypersensitive alarm system, developed from frequent physical or emotional abuse in the past, might be constantly reacting to the environment with fear and anger to the point of being labeled as "paranoid," an overly submissive person responds to the same environment with learned helplessness, and experiences chronic depression.

Animals normally have their alarm systems activated for relatively brief periods and only in response to immediate threat, and at all other times they are generally at rest, in a state of contentment, operating within a relatively safe and nurturing environment. Humans, however, feel constantly challenged by their environment, living in crowded cities, alienated from one another, where the environment can become unpredictably dangerous at any moment. Even within the home, the environment may not be consistently safe, nurturing, and emotionally or physically predictable. Thus, the average person lives constantly in a hostile environment, struggling with inner and outer feelings of alienation, experiencing an increasing pressure of expectations for performance, and competition for survival. Inevitably, the physical body cannot tolerate the stress of continuous mental alienation from a more natural environment, and will gradually break down into a variety of resulting clinical diseases, such as heart disease or cancer, with serious ramifications to the work force including the high cost of medical care in our country, today.

CHAPTER 23(P)

COMPARISON OF THE BRAIN OF

MAN AND DOG

The anatomy of the dog's brain has similar structures to that of the human brain, but with a significant difference in the size of the olfactory lobe (for smell) which is small and slender and well underneath the frontal lobes in man, but well-developed and extending beyond the cerebral hemisphere in dogs. Also the frontal lobes in humans are larger, wider and contain more convolutions or infoldings. The number of convolutions and cresses are related to intellectual power, and there is an increasing complexity of arrangement as one ascends from the lowest mammals up to man.

The five major areas of the brain regulating aggression and violence in humans and higher animals, including the dog are (see diagram: pg. 133).

A. *The Reticular Activating System (RAS)* is situated in the midbrain and brain stem. This is the arousal system which awakens the brain to full alertness.

B. *The Amygdala* is like a central intelligence station which evaluates the nature of all new incoming stimuli from the environment as to whether it is friendly or hostile. Note: the connection of the Amygdala to the Olfactory Bulb (O) suggests that smell, in dogs, is as important as vision in determining the intent of an intruder.

C. *The Limbic System* is a "wishbone" structure encircling the midbrain. This is the "emotional brain," capable of arousing intense anxiety or fear.

D. *The Hypothalamus*, a large structure in the center of the brain, is a sensory switchboard which regulates autonomic functions. When flooded with fear, it stimulates the Sympathetic Nervous System throughout the body to increase heart rate, blood pressure, and muscle tension.

163

E. *The Outer Cortex* (gray matter) comprises the "reasoning" brain. This is especially true of the frontal cortex which is highly developed in humans. Walter Hess (1949) received the Nobel Prize for demonstrating that the cortex is almost totally dependent upon the hypothalamus for instinctual behavioral responses and functioning. However, in humans, the "reasoning brain" has the capacity, when disciplined, to gain mastery over the entire circuitry of the lower centers. For example, it can "order" the amygdala to detect only friendliness, and not a threat, coming from the presence of other humans. It can also be trained to remain calm in a seemingly threatening situation by viewing the situation from a higher or more mature perspective. As the *Course in Miracles* suggests: "You can choose to see love instead of hate."

From the diagram, comparing the brain of dog and man, it is apparent that higher mammals such as the dog (and the cat) have all of the emotional sensitivity of humans, and visa-versa. Thus dogs can feel lonely and are hurt by rejection, and will mourn the loss of an owner. Dogs, in particular, because of their desire to form an emotional bond with humans, take on the emotional energy of their owners and, thus, are prone to suffer from a similar variety of psychosomatic illnesses as do humans.

HOW THE BRAIN WORKS TO
RESPOND TO THE ENVIRONMENT

Aggressive behavior in animals consists of a relatively coordi-nated series of movements which can be evoked by stimulating the brain in the area of the hypothalamus. Such movements include stalking, biting, seizing, shaking, etc. These are stereotyped reactions to a variety of stimuli such as odor, color, rapid movement, or impingement upon the animal's territory by a foreign animal. Aggres-sion is an innate behavior mechanism governing both the patterns of attack for purposes of gaining food, and for the defense of territory. It must be stressed that this behavior is mechanical, unconscious, impersonal, and is relatively consistent and predictable in each species.

In both animals and humans, the brain works like a giant computer to analyze the environment and to respond with a particular behavior pattern. There are some basic components of the computer brain which are routinely brought into operation whenever something new comes into our environment:

One or more of the five senses of perception sends signals to the brain about the environment.

A. *The alerting system* (labeled the Ascending Reticular Activating System, in the brain stem awakens the brain and allows it to focus consciously upon selected stimuli. It also acts to decrease the awareness of constant stimuli, so the brain can ignore them. The vast majority of incoming messages to the brain are subliminal, which means they are kept below conscious awareness. For example, let us imagine that you are absorbed in reading a newspaper on a park bench, when the voice and presence of an approaching stranger startles you. The alerting center brings you to full consciousness and sends a message to a center in the brain called the ...

B. *Amygdala*, which scans the memory patterns of the brain and decides whether this stranger is friend or foe, or someone intending a possibly dangerous violation of your personal space. The amygdala is responsible for setting off a defensive alarm to the ...

C. *Limbic System*, which is the emotional circuitry of the brain. It triggers the emotional experience of agitation, hostility, and fear, while arousing the ...

D. *Hypothalamus*, which chooses a pattern of defensive response, one that is either menacing or submissive. Let us assume the approaching stranger is a police officer, whose reason for approaching you is unknown. In this instance, the brain will most likely choose to activate the submissive response pattern. Your facial muscles flatten and your eyes help promote the appearance of confused passivity. Your lips may crease slightly into a tight, respectful smile. The alarm system keeps firing because the officer's face has a frown and a stare ("attack" mode) and he appears about to say something which you may not want to hear. So the sympathetic nervous system now increases your heart rate, breathing rate, and muscle tension. The experience is as if someone gave you a shot of adrenalin.

The police officer explains that you are parked in a reserved area and must move your car. You jump to oblige. As you drive away, the arousal mechanism begins to subside. It may take several minutes for your pulse to return to normal, especially if the officer's demeanor was curt and the tone of his voice reprimanding.

It is from this point that humans differ from animals in that humans have the mental capacity to replay the experience over and over. Resentment may build up as you consider that the officer's manner was disrespectful. An inner dialogue may continue long after the incident. A part of you might be embarrassed for not realizing you were parked in a restricted area. Another part might briefly consider suing the city for "over-restricting access to land that should be open to the public." Finally, you may release some of your pent-up anger at yourself for having behaved in an overly-submissive way to the officer, by fantasizing your telling him to "Go to hell" — next time.

Because of our advanced intellects, we cannot let go of the little hurts and frustrations of the day, but allow them to fester in our minds, maintaining us in a more or less constant state of emotional upset. In observing animals, I once watched a puppy sniffing about on the lawn. Apparently, he discovered some cookies or other edible morsels tossed there, because his activity took on an appearance of excitement. A larger dog, passing by, took notice and with a menacing growl, took over the smaller dog's find. The smaller dog, with a "Yipe!", surrendered his spot, and without much further ado, proceeded to sniff about in an area some ten feet distant in search of another find.

How differently this would be handled by a human! There would likely be a mental rehearsing of the scene for days or weeks, with attempts to seek recourse, legal or otherwise, for revenge. Mental rehashing of situations perceived as insulting, humiliating, or degrading can evoke physiologic responses in the body equal to the original insult, and can escalate through obsessive dysfunction or, when all recourse is blocked, into clinical depression.

166

CHAPTER 24(P)

CHRONIC STRESS SYNDROME

The fight or flight response triggered by stress causes the release of glucocorticoids. These steroid hormones signal the body to increase blood pressure, heart rate, blood sugar and the flow of blood to the muscles.

In the animal kingdom, this state of high arousal provides a temporary burst of energy to overcome or flee from danger. The body cannot tolerate prolonged periods of such high tension without suffering slow damage to the arteries and organs of the body, and probably, according to recent research, direct damage to the brain cells, as well. This is a common cause of disease and death in our country, today. When there is nothing tangible to fight, the environment itself becomes the challenge. This results in a constant high level of arousal and stress in the struggle for survival in a complex and highly competitive society. The term, "Chronic Stress Syndrome," is gaining acceptance to describe a variety of physical and mental symptoms commonly seen in our medical outpatient clinics, today. Evidence to indicate that major depression may be one end-point of chronic stress is the finding of adrenal glad enlargement in a significant number of people suffering from depression.

When people believe that they cannot influence stressful events, the body lowers its immune response. This may be a clue as to why depression and a sense of helplessness are associated with cancer. In my opinion, it is this and not aggression, as proposed by Freud, that represents the true death instinct in animals and man. The lack of supportive relationships, close family ties, and a strong sense of community is another contributing factor to early death by heart attacks in men, and depression in women. When there is an actual target to fight, an outlet for aggressive energies, there is a concurrent release of tension, replaced by a sense of purpose and significance. During World War II, the incidence of murder, suicide, and other

167

forms of violence was significantly lower than today. When there is no external outlet for frustration, scapegoats are commonly targeted within the society or the family circle to take the blame for frustration, failure, and feelings of helplessness. Who can deny that many of the targets were pre-selected prior to the outbreak of violence in Los Angeles following the Rodney King jury verdict in May of 1992? See graphs, pages 134 - 136.

CHAPTER 25(M)

DEATH PENALTY

for the Innocent

I am hearing from an alarming number of dog owners (and even some trainers) that because of dominant training techniques they have had to destroy their once-loving family dog. Unfortunately, they discovered the 'TRUTH' of why their dog became a Dr. Jekyll & Mr. Hyde after they went through the emotional pain of having their dog killed. The following was written by a breeder who wanted to share her story in order to help prevent others from having to go through the same tragic experience.

NAN AND COMPANIONS

I have been involved very seriously in Ibizan Hounds for over 17 years. Ibizans are generally non-aggressive and amendable, though independent. I never had any accidental breeding until our Catahoulax Heeler farm dog slipped in with Fenix our champion Ibizan Hound on the fifth day of her season. Somehow she managed to bring forth one pure white, blue-eyed lump of a bitch puppy, known as Fcasco, or Moby pup.

I have always been interested in a lurcher, a dog with sight/hound skills but controllable like a herding dog. Fcasco was protectively mothered by Ashley until she was three weeks old at which time Ashley, like a teenage mother, grew bored, leaving Fcasco for me and the Ibizans to raise.

Fcasco grew into a handsome and intelligent dog, racy white body and ice blue eyes, but black nose. She was playful and bright. But at about one year of age she started fighting, mostly with her mother. This went beyond the normal struggle for rank in the pack. I tried traditional reprimands but the situation kept escalating. Fights were getting serious. I'd take her by the collar and shake her, yelling in her

169

face. This only seemed to excite her more. Fcasco walked around the house grumbling like a Japanese monster in a movie.

I re-read all the obedience books, and out came the chain choke. I was advised to lift her off the ground by this after aggressive outbursts. I tried several times. It became clear; I could have killed her and she would not back down. When I threw her in her crate, she turned and showed her teeth. I could not believe with the good temperament of both parents this could happen. Perhaps it was a bad combination of the hair-trigger reflexes of the Ibizan and the bull-headed tenacity of the heeler?

After six months of this I decided on the final solution. We loved Fcasco, but obviously at the rate we proceeded, someone was going to get hurt. It was very difficult, but I was so sure it was the only possible decision. So we had her destroyed.

Then the evil spirit seemed to transfer to Ashley! SHE started fighting and physical correction made her surly. She never bit me, but she warned me when I slapped her under the chin or shook her. It started to look to me like something was deadly wrong here.

Many things about traditional dog training have bothered me — gone against the grain so to speak. Recent years have brought many positive changes, but when a problem arises most books and training institutions still go back to strong physical corrections. It appears to work with many, but some dogs are too soft or too strong-willed. The strong-willed ones often become labeled
as incurable or genetically defective. *These are really often the best dogs*.

I read every new animal book that our wonderful library acquires. There it was — the *Jelly Bean Book*. It sat on my table for two weeks before I finally got to it. I was intrigued by the Dr. Jekyll and Mr. Hyde image set forth. Ironically, we had started to call Ashley 'psycho-dog' due to her erratic behavior.

I read the book from cover to cover, and it totally turned me around in my thinking. Without detailed instructions, just by *not using dominant training methods* and changing my attitude, I found it worked. Taking Ashley firmly by the collar and saying, "no," putting her near me and praising her lack of aggression, her fighting stopped! Soo-simple!! But of course, Ashley is a very smart dog. All tension at feeding time stopped. I was again able to feed every one of my dear companions from their own bowl, at the same time, in the kitchen.

By showing the dogs clearly what I wanted, praising good behavior and simply not allowing the bad, now peace reigns in our home again. Ashley is again the good canine citizen, keeping the livestock in hand and helping to catch chickens on command.

Unfortunately, my ignorance resulted in the loss of a much loved and superior dog — it cost Fcasco's life. I had tried my best. I never intended to harm my dog, but as the saying goes, "The road to hell is paved with good intentions." This was a tragic experience. If I can assist Bill Meisterfeld to prevent future tragedies and regrets, perhaps it was worth it.

Author's comment: Nan informed me that because Ashley was expressing the Dr. Jekyll & Mr. Hyde split personality, she started to believe that it was genetically inherited and was the reason why Fcasco went vicious.

Fortunately, once she stopped using the dominant training methods Ashley (and all her other dogs) returned to the normal behavior of respect, trust, and loyality; the willingness to please/serve their master.

The realization of the true cause of Fcasco's behavioral problems and the unnecessary taking of her life will be a memory that only time will heal.

Thanks Nan for caring and sharing!

CHAPTER 26(M)

DEATH PENALTY

Reprieved

The average dog owner does not have experience in analyzing their dog's behavior. Many of my clients have thoroughly read and researched all of the information that is available on dog behavior, viciousness, and behavior modification, but what baffles many of them is that their dog gets *worse* after following the experts' advice to the letter, such as the following case:

INNIS

(Chris Higgins' story)

I totally agree that physical correction does more harm than good. But after reading an article in a popular dog magazine on How to Train Your Puppy, I have a hard time determining the non-physicality of scruff shakes, or of the fear induced by use of the rattle can or other loud, obnoxious noises. These methods of correction are just as physical as hitting a dog and can just as readily destroy a dog's temperament.

How would a parent feel about these methods if they were used to help teach children in school? Hard shaking of children has been known to produce severe brain damage (see the article "Protect Our Children" in the March 18, 1990 edition of *Parade* Magazine). A dog's brain is no more protected than a child's, and the possibility of damage due to hard shaking is just as strong. A mother dog does indeed correct very young puppies with this method, but she does it very gently, and the practice is replaced by verbal reprimands as the puppies grow up. Have you ever seen an adult dog discipline another adult dog in this manner? What would happen if a wild animal trainer tried to discipline a full-grown Bengal tiger by shaking it by the neck?

173

Psychologists and educators have long acknowledged the ineffectiveness of teaching children by inducing fear. Shake Cans and loud noises interrupt undesirable behavior, at least at first, because they induce fear. Then, one of two things happen. The dog can be so traumatized by fear that he avoids the situation entirely in the future, and you have started on the path to producing a shy, fearful dog; or he becomes accustomed to the noise, and the degree of correction must be continuously escalated to remain effective. It is easy to see that it would not take long before the noise can no longer be increased and the correction loses its effectiveness. Furthermore, all the dog has learned from these methods is that he cannot trust you not to hurt or scare him, and at that point you have a dog that you cannot trust either.

I know whereof I'm speaking. I raised a dog according to the guidelines of the dog establishment, taking him to a puppy kindergarten class, using the recommended rewards and corrections, and treating him like a member of the family. I am a 5 ft., 1 in. tall woman, who weighs 117 pounds, and it was pretty frightening to have an 80 lb. male German Shepherd attack me without warning. Thankfully, I escaped serious injury, but I was devastated that this had happened.

Where had I gone wrong? I was told by an animal behaviorist that he probably had a genetic defect. I was afraid that I would have to have him put to sleep.

Shortly thereafter, I ran across a book with the title, *Jelly Bean versus Dr. Jekyll and Mr. Hyde,* by C.W. Meisterfeld. This book was the first book I had found (and I had read many, many books on the subject) that explained the possible consequences of using dominant correction methods like the scruff shake, Rattle Cans, noises, and the alpha roll-over. Instead, C.W. Meisterfeld recommends the prevention and elimination of problem behaviors by building up a dog's respect and trust in the owner using only positive reinforcement.

I am a graduate student in psychology, working on my doctoral thesis, and thinking about his methods, I began to realize that they are based on sound psychological principles.

With his help, I am now in the process of reprogramming my dog to be a loyal, obedient, and happy companion, one who trusts me and whom I can trust in return.

I can't emphasize strongly enough how important it is for dog owners and trainers to begin to re-examine the dominant training methods that have been so widely disseminated recently. Their effects can be seen in the ever increasing incidents of dog attacks on people, and the ever increasing number of dogs being put to sleep because of behavior problems.

I realize that these methods were designed to help prevent these exact problems, but the simple fact remains that, for many, many dogs, they *just don't work*. Once this is understood, we can begin to train our dogs in the more humane and effective manner that they deserve. Our lives, as well as those of our dogs, will be enriched as a result.

Author's Comment:

What I find most shocking is that dog trainers and dog behavioral experts who have decades of experience do not fully understand dog behavior and are misinforming dog owners. People look to these experts with the expectation of getting accurate and reliable advice which will permit the owners to make life or death decisions in the case of biting and vicious behavior.

I have received many requests for second opinions from dog owners (and trainers) who did not feel right about the *experts*' advice. Such is the following case which took place in my own backyard, thus, I was able to do a hands-on psychological testing and evaluation:

STRONGHEART/GRINGO

(Judy Aziuss' story)

We originally picked up Strongheart in Samuel P. Taylor Park in mid-March. He had been following another couple on the trail for about three hours. They remarked to us on his outgoing friendliness, and a certain unusual awareness they noticed in him. When they got to the top of a mountain, for example, they observed Strongheart to appear to admire the view, and watch the birds flying. When he met other dogs on the trail, he appeared friendly and did not attempt to fight with any of them.

He came into the car with us with some coaxing. He displayed no aggression, but did appear anxious. He talked a lot, making various guttural sounds, and was alert to everything. He spent about 3 hours in our home. He did a lot of pacing. When in the yard, he eyed the fence for escape possibilities. On leash, he was generally not responsive. He didn't seem stubborn, just hyped-up and confused.

The only incident of aggression or fear in the house that day occurred when he saw our cardboard "flat cat" — his fur stood up and he barked at it. He looked afraid.

Strongheart spent more than two months at the Humane Society in Marin County, California. While there, he displayed no aggression. He was friendly with all staff and volunteers. He was always eager for walks and attention. They did, however, observe him to be very escape oriented and aggressive toward cats.

The cat aggression seems debatable, as the local, professional trainers that the Humane Society recommended did not observe him to show an immediate inclination to attack cats or other animals. The exception to this is when Strongheart saw their pet lamb start to run, he tried to chase it. During his week-and-a-half stay at the trainers, cats actually slept on him at times. On the other hand, about two days before we picked him up, apparently, they caught him as he began to lunge at a cat.

The trainers noted that Strongheart already knew some commands. They also observed him to be insecure, but very compliant, highly intelligent, and a fast learner with excellent memory. During the whole week they reported he was very good. In fact, "too good," and they felt that he was hiding something.

I think their method of training involved quick, sharp jerks on the leash. They may also have used the shake can. They also used food as a motivator, and said that he would respond to commands without food. He was always the first at the gate, always wanted to work.

Some of the commands they taught him were: no, no pull, sit, heel, wait, release. They also remarked that Strongheart is a very clean dog, not messing his area and not chewing on things. He was willing to use a crate.

Before the allotted training period was over, an incident occurred that stopped his training with them. They let him off his leash in the house. He made a bee-line for the desk in the office and refused to come out. He bared all his teeth. They told me he was "dangerous" and could never be left off leash, or trusted.

Receiving this news from these expert trainers was unbearable. It was also unthinkable. I couldn't believe that we had gone this far with Strongheart, only to have to put him down. For the previous two months, while he had been at the Humane Society, I had done everything I could to find a home for this amazing animal. And, as his time ran out at the Humane Society, I was finally able to convince my husband, Sam, of what I had felt in my heart all along — that Strongheart was meant to be with us. So, hearing from the trainers that he was not a workable pet was unacceptable.

For several hours Sam and I agonized over what to do. Then I remembered that there is a reputable animal psychic in our county named Penelope Smith. I had no idea what good she could do in this case, but we were grasping for anything that might save our dog, so I called her. She gave me a "reading" on the dog's past, which was interesting, but of course, not verifiable. The other thing she did, though, was to tell me that she felt that Strongheart wanted to be a good dog, and wanted to be part of a family. She suggested that he needed a different kind of training, and gave me Bill Meisterfeld's name. She said that Bill was able to train problem dogs using no pain or fear. So we called him immediately, and he consented to evaluate Strongheart, and then, following evaluation, Bill put both Strongheart and me through his intensive canine behavioral workshop that met for 4 hours every Saturday for 8 weeks. I was surprised to find that most of the attendees also had dog behavioral problems which were directly caused by the dominant training methods that made Strongheart "dangerous."

When I went to get Strongheart from the first trainers, he ran under a car. Finally, with my coaxing, he came out. I also noticed that when I raised my arm to scratch my head, Strongheart became startled and cowered. When we got to Bill's, he emphasized to me that the dog's response of crawling under a desk and growling was not an indication of aggression, but of fear. In other words, this dog had been abused and was trying to defend himself. He was operating on his basic survival instinct.

Retraining Strongheart involved not only time and effort on Bill's part, but time and a great deal of effort on mine. I had to make some important shifts in my attitudes toward the dog, and I learned many lessons along the way. One of the most significant was the meaning of the word, "consistency." But the training process is another whole book.

What I want to say here is, that two years later, Strongheart, who is now transformed to "Gringo," is a wonderful companion. Still a handful — spirited, high energy, insatiably curious and alert. He has also developed trust in me and a willingness to do what I ask of him. I like to call him my Personal Fitness Trainer, because I can take him (on leash) on mountain trails, and he can go forever. He has learned to match my pace, to watch out for barriers, and to pick his way along in places that are difficult for me to negotiate. If I trip or take a spill, he stands by me until I can regain my footing. He is no longer an "escape-oriented" dog.

He has also learned to ignore other animals — cats, dogs, horses, even deer — on command. Sometimes children will pass him and wave their hands in front of his nose, but he remains calm and gentle. Other times we are met by hoards of joggers or bicyclists, and Gringo just sits and allows them to pass by.

At home, Gringo is affectionate and has excellent manners. He never touches food that is on the tables or counter tops. He is protective and will growl or bark when he hears something unusual, but he will also be quiet on command. When I go on errands, I can leave him at home or in the car for as long as a couple of hours without worry. He does not destroy things, but waits patiently for my return.

He is truly a wonderful dog and friend! The effort it took to learn and apply Bill's training methods were well worth it. My beautiful Gringo would have been dead without them.

I wish that other trainers would realize that coercion and fear-inducing methods are not only unnecessary, but actually create problem dogs which must eventually be destroyed. Sure, some of the animals trained under these harsh methods do learn to capitulate and obey. But far too many are like Gringo. They either become so fearful and insecure that they fall apart and become neurotic and unpredictable, or they rebel and become aggressive.

GRINGO

(Sam Case's story)

I remember the morning when I picked up Gringo from the Marin Humane Society to take him to the trainers. On the way out, I met a woman who worked at the Society and told her I was taking the dog to a certain local trainer for training per the Society's recommendation.

"Oh, my!" she exclaimed, "You're going to get a trained dog all right! They are strict. When he comes back from there, he'll be cowering!"

I couldn't tell if she was warning me or being enthusiastic. We had heard that the trainers considered themselves the *top dog trainers* on the West Coast. My wife, Judy and I had taken the dog for an evaluation the previous week and both trainers had impressed us. Strict, but fair, we agreed. And this particular dog did seem to need a firm hand.

Now, however, I began to have more doubts about the whole process of training and adopting the dog. The Humane Society had intimated that this was a potentially dangerous dog. He was big and immensely strong; he looked enough like a German Shepherd to remind me of vicious police dogs. He regarded cats as if they were potential prey. And, at the evaluation, the trainer had talked about electronic collars and electronic fences.

179

On the way up to the trainers, I had visions of high-security prisons: chain link fences topped with barbed wire and guard towers with search lights. The dog would be a prisoner; if he left the grounds, he would always be controlled on a short leash. There would be no playing, no freedom to run around, no coming into the house with the cat.

When I turned around to look at the dog, this grim picture seemed very much out of place. He was his usual friendly self, eager to please and playful, though at the present he was obviously anxious. He whined and looked at the window, came to me to be petted, then turned to the window again. My heart went out to him. Was this a vicious animal?

But, I told myself, what did I know? My main experience with dogs had been the golden retriever I had raised from a puppy when I was a boy. Always friendly, always wanting to please, he would bark at strangers, but just as quickly come to be petted when he learned they were okay. This dog, Gringo, was an unknown. His former owners might have beaten him, for all we knew, or taught him to attack small animals. The experts, the people at the Humane Society and the trainers, must know what they were talking about.

Ten days into the training, our worst fears became real. The trainer called to say that Gringo had parked himself under a desk and refused to come out, growling menacingly if they came near. They had finally gotten him out, but the training was through, as far as they were concerned. This was a "dangerous" dog and could never be let off the leash or fully trusted. I don't know if they actually said it or not, but the feeling was that it would probably be best to euthanize the dog.

Judy and I, needless to say, were extremely upset. We couldn't keep a dangerous dog. Neither could we convince someone to adopt him. At the same time, we had come to have such good feelings for the dog — his intelligence, friendliness, and general "joie de vivre" seemed so special — that the idea of putting him down seemed incredible.

We cast about for some solution for several hours, feeling more and more hopeless. Grasping at straws, Judy finally remembered the name of an "animal psychic," Penelope Smith, and managed to find her phone number.

We got a short "reading" about the dog over the phone, but, more importantly, we were given the name of a different kind of dog trainer, C.W. Meisterfeld, who specialized in problem dogs. Penelope strongly suggested that we call him.

I won't go into detail on the training as it is described in other parts of this book. It has been a long process, though, and one which has put us through more changes than the dog. Although we have now reached a good plateau with the dog, the process is ongoing. He has, as Bill says, a very high "will to power." In the wild, he would be head of the pack. Our main task has been not to attack this will-to-power, but to encourage his "will-to-serve," and show him that we mean what we say.

But we have been able to do this *without* whips and chains, or electric collars and barbed wire fences. Gringo may not be as easy to manage as the retriever I played with as a boy, but over time, we *have* started to play with him. He tears after a tennis ball in the back yard, or leaps up to catch it on a bounce in the house. On walks, he shows very little inclination to fight with other dogs and is invariably friendly to people.

Occasionally, I look at Gringo and think, *this* is a vicious dog? *This* is the dog that the trainers termed "dangerous" and intimated that we should put down? Then I realize that with their kind of harsh training, he *would* have become a dangerous dog. Thousands of dogs do, every year, and thousands are put down because of the way they react to the cruelty of the trainers.

These are "dangerous" people, these trainers. Dangerous people create dangerous dogs. Careful, thoughtful trainers, on the other hand, create the kind of joyful, eager-to-please companions we value so much — Gringo, for example.

ONE QUESTION: WHY?

Judy and I have one question that still remains unanswered . . . WHY??? The Humane Society *did not* give us Meisterfeld's name as a second choice. We both find it hard to believe that they were not aware of Bill, especially since he has appeared on every T.V. and radio talk show in the San Francisco Bay Area. He also has been featured several times in the *San Francisco Chronicle and Examiner*, plus he has been operating his dog training center and specializing in dog behavioral problems for over 25 years, just 30 miles away. Recently, we have seen the training booklet that is published by the Humane Society which may explain the WHY? to our question. The training booklet talks about such disciplinary methods as how to properly give your dog a scruff shake, and how to correctly hit him under the jaw with enough force to cause his head to snap back.

Author's Comment:

When I psychologically tested Strongheart, the level of fear of being handled was very high. He was on a constant red-alert, operating mainly on his survival/adrenal system. Also, his very high ability to discriminate, coupled with an extraordinarily high intelligence, enabled him to figure things out to the point of reasoning. This unique personality makeup is what the trainers erroneously considered "too good" and caused them to feel that he was hiding something.

What these training experts were witnessing was Strongheart's awareness of the abusive dominant training they were using on him and his having to comply with it. That is, until he was able to hide under the table in order to protect himself.

The other aspect of Strongheart that the trainers didn't understand was that he had a very high servitude and willingness to please, and to work, which was the main reason he did not rebel in the earlier days.

CHAPTER 27(P)

EVALUATING THE CAUSES

OF DISRUPTIVE BEHAVIOR

Naturalists who study the behavior of animals, birds, and insects have arrived at some clearly defined and predictable patterns for each species around feeding, mating, raising the young, and adaptive responses to the environment. Human behavior, on the surface appears to be far more complex, but if we reduce the variables by focusing on the category of socially acceptable (conforming) versus socially unacceptable (non-conforming) behaviors, we can make some useful observations.

Behavior, from its simplest definition, is a definable activity or action. Our attitudes and our reactions to a particular behavior by others are colored by the subjective judgments we make regarding the motives which prompted the behavior. Once we label a behavior as "willful disobedience," "insane," "manipulative," "uncaring," hostile," "selfish," etc., we then react to the label and to the "attitude" that usually fits that label. For example, a child may spill milk on the floor and the parent will react according to their interpretation, ranging from "innocent accident," or, "careless indifference," to "an act of defiance." Most of the arguments between married couples are due to the negative misinterpretation of motives and to the counter attacks that result from being wrongly accused. It requires considerable training to refrain from projecting one's own insecurity and motives upon the behavior of others and to assume a totally objective stance. This is, of course, more easily accomplished with animals than with children, but even here emotionalism can often interfere with training.

Every society establishes its own set of rules regarding the expression of social behaviors so as to avoid misinterpretation. These become part of the customs and norms of the society. They represent a consensus as to what constitutes appropriate or polite behavior, eccentric but acceptable behavior, or deviant, non-conforming, and unacceptable behavior. *A behavior is labeled as aggressive behavior whenever it results in making an impact upon the environmental space of another person.* The result is usually some degree of annoyance even when it's only giving to someone an unanticipated hug. It may not even be directed at you. A child's loud talking or screaming in a restaurant may elicit feelings of annoyance rising gradually to anger, especially if you tell yourself that the behavior is "entirely inappropriate" and, furthermore, "the result of poor manners."

There is a natural propensity in all living organisms to express periodically innate aggressive patterns of behavior, even if it is in the form of play. In general, the more civilized the culture, the more restricting and limited are aggressive options against any type of provocation. Society decides which aggressive behaviors are justifiable and which are not. For example, in some countries, the social order may sympathize with your shooting a man you find in bed with your wife, however, you are not permitted to punch his nose for taking your parking space.

The outer world is always in opposition to our will, even in a "free society." We are always struggling with the inner option of conformance versus rebellion. Every stable culture instills habits, rituals, and customs in its citizenry which lead to comfortable, mechanically appropriate interactions within the population. So long as this includes a sense of security, adequate opportunities to maintain a livelihood, and a sense of justice, the likelihood for outbreaks of violence will be minimized. Thus, the management of aggression, in a way that maintains the security of the territorial boundaries of each individual member, is the primary task of every democracy, every superintendent of a school, institution, or prison, every military commander, and every head of a family. Aggression, improperly contained, and lacking the control of a disciplined mind, eventually provokes counter-aggression and widespread violence.

FREUD

Sigmund Freud based his original theories of behavior upon the instincts governing pain and pleasure. However, when World War I broke out, he was at a loss to explain the wanton bloodshed he witnessed. This led him to postulate another instinct, which he labeled "thanatos," the death instinct. It is amazing to me how he could have missed the obvious: War is not the result of any natural instinct; *war is the result of man's reasoning mind!* It is man's reasoning mind which makes him far more dangerous than any other animal, and far more destructive to himself, his neighbors, and to the planet. His reasoning mind is quite capable of convincing itself to kill millions of other people as a service to God!

There actually is a death instinct in animals which prevents unnecessary suffering and which involves the cessation of all aggression and a withdrawal of the life force. Thus, animals held unhappily in captivity will die regardless of how well their physical needs are met. This is a common occurrence in humans as well. It is well documented that men often die shortly after retirement, and senior citizens after the death of a beloved mate, and when life no longer seems to have any meaning.

In order to understand the causes and cures for violence, we must understand the difference between aggression and violence. All aggression does not lead to violence. Even when aggression results in death, it is quantitatively and qualitatively different than the killing that is labeled as violence.

The innate mechanisms governing aggressive behavior and those which promote violence have some important and distinct differences in the mammalian and human brain. The aggressive center is periodically and spontaneously activated for both attack and for play. It is not motivated by either anger or fear, but by a hunting instinct for food, and by a natural need for physical expression and interaction. It is often associated with a feeling of exhilaration ("adrenal rush"), but this rarely results in an excessive use of force or an intent to cause unnecessary suffering.

Every society offers acceptable outlets for aggression, and its expression may be rewarded with money or praise when it is accompanied by a demonstration of skill or courage. There are always special conditions placed upon it, along with the expectation that its execution will be disciplined and controlled. Again, this may or may not involve killing, but in all cases there is a prohibition against the use of excessive force.

Socially Condoned Aggression

A. All sporting events (regulated by detailed rules)
B. Hunting (in season)
C. Bull-fighting (within an arena)
D. Animal slaughter (for food)
E. The death penalty (by jury)
F. Military killing (when ordered)
G. Felony killing (by police when necessary)
H. Child spanking (if unemotional)
I. Animal killing (at specified Pounds)

Needless to say, all of the above are occasionally questioned by humane and special interest groups as to their appropriateness. In any event, excessive force is always denounced. Even when achieving a military objective, such as in the Gulf War, the possible misuse of excessive force is still being debated. Aggression involving undue pain and suffering is also unacceptable. Hence, cock fighting is declared illegal in this country. The initial protest against the Vietnam War was not motivated by its high cost in money nor by loss of military personnel, nor by its dubious political value to this country, but by the leadership's mentality that kept score by "kill ratio." The earliest protesters carried placards saying, "Stop the killing!"

Even the asocial or criminal use of aggression is also characteristically unemotional and concerned more with "precision" than blood-letting. We may label it "cold-blooded murder" because the associated emotions are no different than that of a hunter in killing a deer. Examples include premeditated murder for personal gain by relatively intelligent and successful people, not unlike the villains characterized in the popular detective "Columbo" television series. A hit-man for the "mob" was once interviewed on television with a mask over his face. Rather than remorse, he expressed pride in his profession.

Only recently are we becoming aware of the capacity of the average person to commit acts of aggression when following the orders of a person in authority. Adolph Eichmann who masterminded the holocaust which resulted in the death of millions of Jews in World War II, was kidnapped by the Israeli secret service, Mossad, and taken to Israel in 1962. There, he was administered a battery of psychological tests with surprising results. He passed as perfectly normal in every respect, including attitudes toward family and social mores. Since that time, a number of research studies have shown that volunteers will readily administer excruciatingly painful shocks to innocent subjects at the command of the person in charge. The lesson to be learned here is that even "normal" aggression can be lethal if misdirected and not restrained by a sense of personal conscience.

Violence, on the contrary, almost always involves an excessive use of force, is motivated by fear and rage, and relishes the eliciting of pain and suffering. Violence is provoked by an activation of the fight or flight survival center in the brain as diagrammed earlier. While aggression is an expression of the attack mode from a position of relative strength, violence is the end-point of the brain's defensive mechanisms against a perceived threat to the integrity of the self-system. Rage floods the sensorium to obliterate fear. This is accompanied by the release of adrenalin and other hormonal substances which brings the body to a high level of alertness, tension, and reactivity. The sympathetic nervous system races the heart and shunts blood to the voluntary muscular system.

In the animal kingdom, there is a relatively rapid resolution of this high tension state through a climactic encounter or a successful flight. However, in humans, the body may be maintained in a relative state of tension for extended periods of time. In fact, this is becoming more commonly a part of the human condition. Chronic stress leads to a premature breakdown of the physical body, and the most common cause for rising medical costs today. It can result in chronic fatigue and depression. In young males it may be experienced as an inner "powder keg," ready to explode.

The important understanding here is that the aggressive mode is rarely stressful. It certainly can be strenuous, but can still be categorized as recreation. When you feel in charge and in control, and experience a sense of excitement rather than fear, there is relatively little build-up of tension. This is a proactive mode that is compatible with a sense of health and well-being.

Stress results from the defensive mode, the fight or flight mode, and especially when you can't run and can't fight. The now familiar Type-A personality who dies of a heart attack in his early fifties is constantly in the defensive mode. He is angrily and impatiently battling other people, fighting against time, and in conflict with himself.

The graphs on page 134 and page 135 compare the normal stress patterns of animals in their natural habitat with that of a human trying to survive in a stressful and competitive environment.

The way the body was meant to cope with stress in the animal kingdom is that each challenge is handled to completion before the next, without a residual build-up of tension. In animals, there is a natural, rapid restoration of physiologic mechanisms to normal resting levels following a crisis. However, with human behavior, even the relatively normal pace of living in the big city of a technological society can lead to a progressive increase in the state of tension over time resulting in high blood pressure, headaches, insomnia, chronic irritability, any number of psychosomatic illnesses and even death.

It's the "Termites" that Weaken the Structure

Some of the little things that eat away at us are:
   Burnt dinner
   Dislike of job
   Marital problems
   Child has school problems

Argument with in-laws
Another speeding ticket
Elderly parent hospitalized
Re-injury of lower back
Funeral of a close friend/relative
Pet dog bites neighbor child
Reprimanded by the boss
Spouse admits infidelity
Constantly required to work overtime
Unwanted pregnancy
Credit card balance soaring
Dog constantly digging up the lawn
Argument with child over curfew
Dog chews on furniture
Continuing health problems of a child/loved one
Disagreements over how to raise the children
Sexual harassment at work or in public
Disagreements with spouse over financial priorities
Guilt, or being blamed for the past
Worry about the future

I can remember my disbelief when a retired member of the Green Berets, a highly trained special forces group in the Vietnam War who frequently engaged in extremely dangerous operations behind enemy lines, stated in a television interview that he found much more stressful the day-to-day frustrations and challenges of living in a major city. He explained that during wartime, his forays into enemy territory were dangerous but exhilarating, and left him with a sense of a completed mission. And there was always sufficient time allowed in between each operation for rest and full recovery before the next. Since he returned home, "the stress level never recedes." Aggressive activity is not stressful, even when strenuous. Much worse is the build-up of unreleased tension and the feeling of helplessness associated with facing an overwhelming accumulation of little problems which don't go away. Like termites they slowly weaken and destroy the infrastructure of the body and the mind.

Sadly, the highly touted, incredibly expensive medical system in this country does essentially little more than keep the individual patched together or heavily tranquilized with pills to temporarily postpone the inevitable.

The Japanese have a word for it: "Karoshi" — death by overwork. Tens of thousands of Japanese men are dying prematurely from heart attacks and strokes each year due to the competitive pressures put on them for advancement. Attorney Hiroshi Kawahito, head of the National Defense Council for Victims of Karoshi, claims that the health of over ten million Japanese men who work 58 hour weeks without vacations or holidays are being sacrificed to the Japanese work ethic.

CHAPTER 28(M)

THE POLYGRAPH DOES NOT LIE

In his *Bodily Changes in Pain, Hunger, Fear and Rage* (1929), Walter Cannon outlined his thesis about the utility of physiological changes accompanying emotional arousal as being part of a primitive flight or fight survival response. He noted that the physiological organs of both humans and animals are constructed to allow them to mobilize for emergencies. He reasoned that in times of stress, threat or emotional upheaval, the body has to have the adaptive capacity either to flee or to fight for survival.

The adrenalin secreted in times of stress cooperates with the sympathetic nerve impulse system. Thus, it floods the blood with sugar. It helps to distribute the blood to the heart, lungs, central nervous system and limbs, while taking it away from inhibited organs of the abdomen. It quickly abolishes the effects of muscular fatigue and renders the blood more rapidly coagulable.

These remarkable, basic physiological responses are common to both man and dog. The elementary experiences of fear, pain, and rage happen suddenly in critical situations. (*The Language of the Heart* by James J. Lynch.)

When the polygraph was first tested in 1922 under controlled laboratory conditions, the dog was used as a guinea pig because of his similar flight or fight (survival) responses to certain stimuli. The heart rate rose; the pulse frequency increased when the dog was suddenly introduced to a loud noise. Yet, present popular dog training methods teach the dog owner to yell at his dog or scream at him. For those who do not have sufficient lung power to scream, the advice is to fill a can with gravel or pennies and throw it near the dog when he is misbehaving. Of course, this will startle the pet and produce temporary results, since a dog's hearing is 5-6 times more powerful than ours.

In field training a hunting dog, the owner is advised by the author to *"Blow a whistle as loud as you can — if possible, into the dogs ear to discipline him for unwanted behavior."* This is another distinct example of shock and fear conditioning.

With the dog's excellent hearing ability, he perceives loud and sudden noises, such as yelling, shouting, rattling, etc., as a threat triggering the fear/defense reflex in him. Blowing an ear-piercing whistle into his extremely sensitive ears can drive a dog paranoid.

Loud, unexpected noises in general are not only disagreeable for a dog, but he associates them with negative events, such as danger and pain. The result can be either escape or aggression — resulting in biting.

How do loud, startling noises and high-pitched whistles affect you?

In order to demonstrate and better understand what the dogs' physiological responses are at the moment of being startled, I had a young lady play guinea pig, substituting for our dogs. It was amazing that even though she fully understood we were only role-playing and I was not really angry with her, her physiological responses of flight and fight were promptly triggered . . . Yes, the polygraph does not lie.

REPRIMAND
With an Angry Tone of Voice

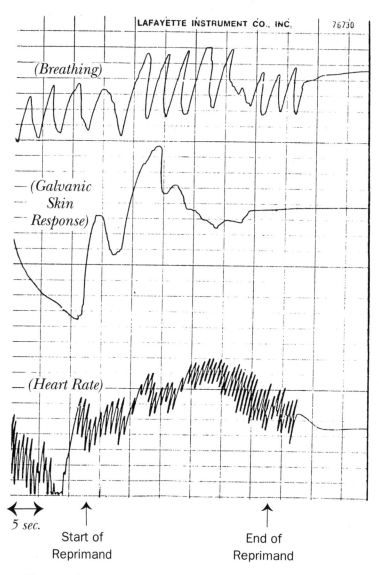

(Breathing)

(Galvanic Skin Response)

(Heart Rate)

5 sec.

Start of Reprimand

End of Reprimand

According to Leonard Saxe, a professor of psychology at Boston University and principal author of a 1983 study on polygraph validity for the Congressional Office of Technology Assessment, "The polygraph doesn't detect lies, it records such telltale signs of anxiety as increased pulse, breathing and perspiration."

NONVERBAL REPRIMAND
Finger Pointing

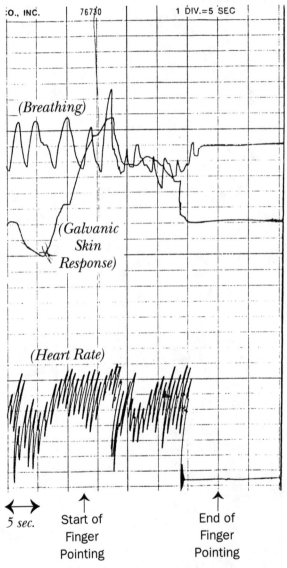

Considering the impact of nonverbal finger pointing at a person, it becomes obvious how much a dog is negatively affected by any threatening body gesture.

Dr. Albert Mehrabian, a noted researcher in the field of nonverbal communication (UCLA) found that only 7% of our feelings and attitudes are communicated with words, 38% via tone of voice and 55% through nonverbal expressions.

POSITIVE CORRECTION
With a Soft Tone of Voice

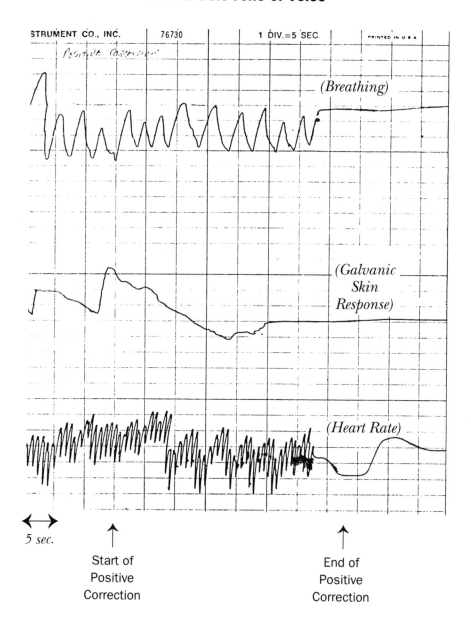

STRUMENT CO., INC. | 76730 | 1 DIV.=5 SEC. | PRINTED IN U S A

Positive Correction

(Breathing)

(Galvanic Skin Response)

(Heart Rate)

5 sec.

Start of
Positive
Correction

End of
Positive
Correction

195

CHAPTER 29(P)

THE ANGER TO VIOLENCE SYNDROME

The anger-to-violence syndrome describes a relatively rapid series of events in which an apparently stable situation becomes rapidly volatile, and a seemingly minor encounter suddenly escalates to violence. Sometimes the tightly coiled spring of anger is released by a sudden trigger without prior warning upon an otherwise innocent target, and after the release there may be guilt and remorse. There is a characteristic curve to this anger-to-violence syndrome seen especially in many wife-beaters, child-beaters, and disturbed adolescents. The violence is not premeditated. However, one or more individuals are predisposed to a low stress tolerance by a prior build-up of tension over the previous hours, days, or months.

Angere to Violence Stages/Levels (see page 136 — "Going Off")

1. One individual has his alarm system on high, which results in a state of mild paranoia. He gives off warning signals by acting irritable or moody. His earlier attempt to calm his nerves with a couple of beers only makes the situation worse by lessening his restraint and self-control.

2. A triggering event, usually in the form of a criticism, angry retort, or even a non-verbal gesture portraying disgust or rejection pushes a "button," an old, unhealed wound from the past.

3. He reacts defensively for a fleeting moment, then suddenly experiences his blood rushing to his head filled with rage. He counterattacks angrily, like a cornered animal.

4. His attack is met with a threat, an argument, or, even worse, by kidding or mockery from bystanders who are unaware of his now brittle condition.

5. He has reached, in his own mind, the absolute limit of what he can tolerate in terms of abuse and humiliation.

6. This brings him to a critical point to where he has only a split-second to shut down the whole system and leave, or to allow his

197

instinctive survival mechanism to take over. His heart is pounding from adrenalin. His stomach is gripped in a knot. Rage is obliterating his fear. The beer he drank now makes it impossible to maintain control.

7. His body erupts into a flurry of violent movements with a deadly focus upon the intent of doing as much harm as possible with whatever means or weapons are available to him.

8. He is now legally and clinically in a state of "temporary insanity." Bystanders who attempt or try to restrain him are met with the full force of his fury. (Police who attempt to break up a domestic quarrel at this point are at high risk of becoming the target of a lethal attack.)

9. The release of rage through exhaustive discharge gradually restores his rational thinking processes. With this comes a slow comprehension and re-evaluation of his behavior.

10. This may result in guilt and an attempt to justify the attack to others, *i.e.*, "I was driven to it," or to extreme remorse and depression. Adolescents may have to be watched for suicidal behavior following an act of violence.

The above scenario is characteristic of those which result in wife-beating. Some husbands may plead with their wives the next day — "Please forgive me, I didn't mean it. Please don't leave me." — while the majority will go into denial and will try to pretend that it never happened.

I have worked with couples in marriage counseling in which the husband reaches stage six (above) and, sensing his loss of self-control, will attempt to leave the house. The wife, however, suffering from abandonment fears, blocks his exit, pleading to "talk it over." This, more often than not, results in her becoming the subject of assaultive behavior.

ASSESSING VIOLENCE POTENTIAL

Violence potential differs in everyone and is dependent upon a number of factors including genetic temperament and personality traits, early childhood traumas, exposure to modeling of violence in the home or in the community, and current environmental stress. Still, after careful consideration of all of these factors, the best predictor of violence is a previous history of violence. This is because, in humans, it involves an inner decision to allow an emotionally irrational, instinctive survival mechanism to take over control of the body, and each time permission is given, the lesser become the constraints against future consent.

There may be genetic traits which predispose some males to criminality and which can be detected by the third grade. They compulsively engage in aggressive, disruptive behavior regardless of consequences, as if they have little or no self-control. Many of these fit the diagnostic category of Attention Deficit Disorder with Conduct Disturbance.

Drs. Ervin and Mark at Massachusetts General Hospital, in Boston, described some 25 years ago, the Dyscontrol Syndrome in men who often had abnormal brain waves. These men, probably a small but significant percentage of our male population, can be triggered into rage at the slightest provocation. In a typical incident, one man went out of control with rage when someone pulled in front of his car on the freeway. He chased the car for two miles, honking wildly, and finally forced it off the road. He got out, smashed the front door window, and was wrestling with the driver when police intervened.

Because of the easy availability of guns, the violent attack upon a pre-selected target presents a major social problem. Over the past ten years, a profile of individuals with a high potential for violence reveals some fairly consistent findings. They are frequently the product of a family marked by frequent brutality and inappropriate fathering. Their fathers are either absent or cruel and abusive. Their mothers are usually brittle, insecure, and highly emotional. As children, they tend to be loners, do not know how to play, and express very little feeling. They have low-average intelligence and poor academic achievement. They feel left out of the social structure, are extremely jealous of other children, and have poor control over their impulses. The most consistent deficit is in communication skills, which contribute to their inability to maintain interpersonal relationships. They are commonly out of touch with feelings, but will often complain of physical symptoms, such as headaches or "something wrong with my body."

In general, deprivation of social contact coupled with deficits in communication skills result in the highest potential for violence. These individuals have a pervasive sense of inadequacy, a paranoid orientation toward the environment, and extreme sensitivity to criticism, rejection, and humiliation.

VIOLENCE IS A LEARNED BEHAVIOR

In recent years the view that violence is a learned form of social behavior is gaining wider acceptance. Today, violence is indirectly promoted by the media as an acceptable option to solve a variety of problems. Aggressive behavior is commonly linked to a positive masculine self-image. Aggression is rewarded in sports, glorified by war, and materially rewarding through crime. Violence, when portrayed on television and in movie scenes evoking fear and horror, arouse a stimulating adrenal response primarily in men where often there is an arousal of sexual stimulation, as well. Many of the most popular movies consist of the basic theme: a hero or heroine being thrown back upon basic survival instincts through attack by alien or evil forces and which is handled through raw counter-violence until the enemy is destroyed, revenge is complete, and security is restored.

The world of the entertainment media is portrayed as consisting largely of selfish, power-hungry, unconscionable men and women against whom there are no options other than kill or be killed. The more humane traits of compassion, receptivity and trust are not only seen as ineffective, but when initially portrayed by the hero or heroine, they are changed later by the realization that counter-violence is the only realistic option for survival.

TELEVISED VIOLENCE

Learning theory very definitely implicates the movie industry and the mass media as provocateurs of violence. Research with children and adults clearly shows that viewing violence increases the drive to engage in violent acts.

Probably the two major factors contributing to the increase of violence in this country today is the combination of environmentally induced frustration coupled with increasing exposure to violent models in the home, in the streets, and on the television screen. Research over the past 25 years shows that there is a definite correlation between aggressive behavior in children and exposure to televised violence, and that the effect is accumulative over time. The effect is three-fold:

1. An identification with the hero who resorts to violence and who glorifies violence as a way of extracting justice.

2. There is a decrease in the restraint against using violence as an option.

3. There is a progressive desensitization to the pain and the suffering of others.

STRESS-RELATED VIOLENCE

The environment provided by our largest cities is filled with stress-inducing factors, including pollution (odor, smog, irritants), a high noise level, and crowding, all of which is known to have profound deleterious effects upon animals held in captivity. Social frustrations due to unemployment, inability to cope with competition, harassment, and provocation among ethnic groups, poor self-concept — all contribute to a feeling of social alienation in our adolescent population most responsible for violent crimes. However, the resort to violence is still based upon learned behavior. In most people, frustration leads to depression. The triad of frustration-depression-anger underlies the growing level of stress in our general population and makes us high users of tranquilizers, anti-depressants, and expensive medical services for stress-related illness. A high level of frustration leads to the seeking of non-specific targets for a release of tension. The high level of tension under which the average person operates can be examined by the level of impatience and tolerance seen on our freeways.

If a senior citizen drives too slowly, or pulls blindly in front of another car or delays at a stop light after the light has turned green, how will the car behind respond? How often have you been the passenger in a car driven by a man who continually criticizes and cusses the drivers in front of him? Honking can serve as a warning much as the growl of a dog. Angry, loud honking with the intent of startling, embarrassing, and reprimanding the driver of the other car constitutes an act of non-physical violence.

CHAPTER 30(M)

RAGE

Dr. Jekyll & Mr. Hyde

There are various levels of rage in dog behavior. Some of it can be understood by comparing human behavior, and some rage is outside of human behavior patterns.

CAUSES

1. Catering and placating the dog.
2. Using the dog for a child substitute.
3. Using the dog for an emotional human companion substitute.
4. Inconsistency in behavioral boundaries/requirements.
5. Dominant/forceful training methods that cause anger and fear, which activates the surging of adrenals for the flight or fight mechanism (survival).

This can have a very negative and damaging effect on a dog that has been trained to behave within certain defined behavioral boundaries. Inconsistency creates a double standard which the dog's minds is not capable of rationalizing.

My first experience (and almost my last) was in 1963. I will never forget the dog's name, Pierre. Ironically, this 10-pound miniature poodle was the catalyst for my becoming a canine psychoanalyst. He also caused me to seriously consider returning to the Ohio winters which I had recently left behind.

Pierre's owners informed me that he was a very loving dog and that he had only one little behavioral problem. The problem was, when Pierre was left alone too long at home, he would go into a rage and destroy whatever was closest to him. One time he destroyed his own wicker basket bed and mattress. Another time he got into the closet and destroyed several pairs of shoes. Another time he chewed up the legs on the coffee table. Yet, as long as he had human companionship he did not chew or destroy anything.

I took Pierre on for a four-week training period. I worked him for 20-30 minutes, four times a day. At this time, I was still living in an apartment. When I was sleeping he was required to sleep in his own dog bed in the kitchen. I ignored the few times that he had found something to chew on in the kitchen. During the day I put him outside in a kennel run. After a week of working with Pierre, he stopped his chewing and did not chew anything for the next three weeks.

As I demonstrated the basic obedience commands Pierre had willingly learned, I felt elated and thought I had made a good move by leaving the Ohio weather and settling in the West. California really looked golden to me in more ways than one.

Three weeks later I received a phone call from Pierre's owners. He had started to chew on things again when he was left alone. "Bring him back free of charge," was my response. I thought that maybe I hadn't kept him long enough to instill his new behavior.

Again Pierre willingly accepted his place in the kitchen and the daily obedience workout. This time when I turned Pierre over to the owners I recommended that they too train him every day and put him through the obedience commands, which he enjoyed doing. Both the husband and wife were pleased with Pierre's willingness and quick response to their commands. Everyone had left happy.

Approximately three weeks later, another phone call came in from Pierre's owners asking if I would meet them in the San Anselmo shopping center. When I asked if Pierre had started chewing again, they would not answer my question. The man's voice was foreboding, but I felt I had to go. As I drove into the parking lot, they were both waiting for me alongside their Rolls Royce. The wife was holding Pierre and as I got closer the husband beckoned me to look inside the car door. What I saw has left an imprint in my mind that I will always remember. The door panel, the front seats, the sunvisors, and the padding on the dashboard was chewed up and torn to shreds. It must have taken a couple of minutes for me to realize that I was looking at the remains of a 10-pound dog's rage. Then I was informed that all of this destruction was done in less than half an hour.

I was dumbfounded and speechless. The only thought that ran through my mind was, can I break the lease with the person renting my home and kennel in Ohio and return? Can I convince my old clients that I will stay once I return? Can I get my position back with the pheasant clubs where I was hired to rent my German Shorthair Pointers for hunting and taking people on guided trips? As the owners were talking I was thinking about leaving this state and its crazy dogs (even though Pierre was my first experience here in California, at the time I felt that one was enough).

Surprisingly, the owners were not expressing any anger and once I realized this, my mind stopped racing. To show them I was interested in what had happened, I asked them where Pierre had been sleeping. To this they replied, "Under the covers. He even snores at times." The next question I asked them was where he eats, to which they replied, "Why, he eats with us. He has his own chair with a cushion and I feed him with a fork after I have cut up his meat for him." When I heard that, I snapped out of my mental shock. I told them that if they made him sleep in a dog's bed and eat out of a dog's dish on the floor that maybe he would not revert from his training after he's with me. Then as I was trying to get out of this ego-deflating predicament, they told me that they wanted me to train him again. Before Pierre started his destructiveness, he had been very obedient and loving.

I was very reluctant to even consider it, but eventually agreed to retrain him with the condition that they follow my training advice and commands exactly. They would no longer be able to let Pierre sleep with them or sit at the table. He was to eat out of his own dish on the floor. They agreed to this so Pierre went through 8 weeks of training. Once again, the owners training sessions (which I extended to three visits) went very smoothly and all departed happy.

Two weeks later, I expected to receive their phone call. Three weeks went by — not a word. Before the fourth week came, I decided I couldn't stand it any longer. I called and asked them how Pierre was doing. I was expecting a damage report, but they stated that he was fine and that he seemed to enjoy sleeping alone and eating out of his own dog dish on the floor. Also, he had never attempted to chew on anything when we left him alone. How ironic that my present profession was hinged on a 10-pound poodle which also could have been the cause of my return to the winters in Ohio.

From this experience I learned the importance of environmental conditioning, and the relationship owners form with their dogs, such as child substituting and humanization (which I coined back then).

A more severe case of rage was an old English Sheepdog that I had reprogrammed due to his aggressive behavior toward strangers and motorcyclists. Because the owners did not adhere to the behavioral ground rules I had believed were necessary to keep their dog, Goliath, mentally balanced, Goliath turned into a raging, vicious dog any time he did not get his way. The following story could have been written many times over using various dogs I have reprogrammed from toys and mutts to hunting breeds and Great Danes:

GOLIATH

I wondered what might have gone wrong with Goliath. Diana hadn't said over the phone, although I could tell she was upset. But I would find out soon enough because she was due at any moment. As I waited for her, I though back to the first time she'd brought her 150-pound Old English Sheepdog in for training.

"I do hope he'll be all right." Diana said to me after I'd put the dog in the run.

I smiled. "Oh, don't worry about *him*. The question is, are *you* going to be all right?"

Diana laughed. "Well, I have to admit that I'll probably miss him, even if he *is* a pain in the you-know-what most of the time. But I'm grateful that you're going to teach him some manners for me. I don't know why he loves to chase people on bicycles like he does." Diana raised her skirt slightly, revealing skinned and bandaged knees. "I can't take any more of this. He drags me around on the leash like a rag doll. Maybe if he didn't outweigh me by forty-five pounds I could handle him. But as it is, I'm bruised and sore in places I never knew

I had before. I'm afraid to let go because he might run off and not come back or something."

"Does he give your husband the same trouble?"

"No, my husband has very little time for him actually. Oh, he romps with Goliath when he gets a chance and isn't too tired. But that's about all. The two boys play with him too — when they're around. You know how teenagers are; to them home is just a pit-stop. They come in, refuel, maybe rest, then they're off again." Diana shrugged her shoulders and smiled. "So it's just Goliath and me, mainly. That's why I had to think of some way for me to control him. And that's why I'm here."

Goliath's initial training had proved to be highly successful. I remembered how happy Diana was when the time came for her to take him home.

"There are three things that you're going to have to watch with him," I had told her in the last training session. "Number one, Goliath has a strong will-to-power and is aggressive by his own nature. Number two, you have to maintain the master-dog relationship we have now established; that means correcting him the *first* time he attempts any old behavior pattern. Number three, you cannot use him for an emotional substitute."

Diana understood.

"And remember, if you have any questions later on, don't hesitate to call." She said that she would.

A month later, Diana pulled into the parking lot of the kennel and soon she was sitting once again in my office with Goliath. I looked down at him and shook my head. He looked terrible. He had a wild, unfocused look in his eyes, which shifted nervously about the room. He was panting heavily and his tongue lolled out the side of his mouth.

"What's been happening since he left here?"

Diana shifted uneasily in her chair. She swallowed hard and from beginning to end, told me the whole story . . .

"When I drove home after our last session together, I was so thrilled about having a trained, obedient dog. In fact, I tried to remember everything you told me during our sessions so that I wouldn't make any mistakes in handling him. The next morning, before the rest of the family dispersed, I demonstrated the things Goliath and I had learned. Jim and the boys thought it was great. I was so proud!

"That afternoon as I got ready to take Goliath for a walk, I decided to go by way of the bicycle route. That's the one place I never dared take him before and I was a little scared. There were no bikes in sight as we approached the path, and I was greatful for that. After a while I spotted a bicycle approaching in the distance. Goliath saw it too. Just as it whirred past, Goliath made a lunge for it. I said, *"NEIN,"* and jerked on the leash as hard as I could. That surprised him, I think, because he got back into the heel position right away. I was shaking slightly but I realized that I had actually stopped him. The next time a bicycle approached, he checked with me before responding to it. I made it clear that he was to leave it alone, and he did. By the end of our walk I didn't even have to warn him to behave when a bike went by. In a couple of weeks, he'd lost interest in them altogether.

"He never got over his love of sprawling all over the furniture though. I gave him a special bed in one corner of the living room, but he didn't seem to like it. I caught him up on the couch several times with the boys, even though they knew I didn't want him up there. But he always got down when I told him to. Then the boys would start in. 'Aw, Mom, he's not hurting anything.' Well, after going through this so many times, my resistance began to crumble. Goliath had been so well-behaved in every other way, that as a reward I finally let him up on the couch. He seemed to be content with that for a while, but then started to beg to get up on our bed. Before I knew it, he was up on the furniture all the time. But . . . I let it go," she said wistfully.

"One day I noticed that Goliath had gotten very interested in motorcycles. He'd sit at the front room window watching for them to come by so he could bark at them. I felt uneasy about that but I couldn't get him to stop. I should have called you about it, but I thought I could work it out somehow. I was very careful walking him and if I heard a motorcycle coming, I would try to avoid it by stepping off onto a side street or something. But one day I let my mind drift and didn't hear the motorcycle through the usual traffic sounds. It came up behind us and before I knew it, I was on the ground. Goliath dragged me right out into the street. I was terrified and tried to let go of the leash but my hand was completely through the loop. I thought I was as good as dead because the cars were zooming past, honking their horns. A young man walking by saw me and ran to help. He caught Goliath and helped me to the sidewalk. That was the last time I ever walked him. I left him out in our small backyard from then on.

"After that episode, I decided to go back to the old rules, but Goliath no longer obeyed me. It wasn't that he questioned my authority, he ignored it completely. But I persevered, hoping I would regain control if I worked him faithfully. Still, he refused to get off the furniture since I'd told him it was okay.

"One night I made his food and gave it to him. I went through the whole routine of making him sit and stay until I said it was okay for him to eat. Well, he dug in as he always does, and I noticed that the food was starting to spill out over the side of the dish, so I went and got a newspaper to put underneath it. As I got near him I heard a deep growl. Goliath had his head low to the dish and he was staring at me. He growled again to let me know he meant business. I called Jeff over and asked him to walk slowly toward Goliath. The dog growled at him too. He became increasingly intolerant of us when he was eating, until we couldn't get within ten feet of him. Finally I'd mix his food, put it in the laundry room, shove Goliath in after it and shut the door until he was finished.

"My breaking point came one hot afternoon. I was planning a small dinner party for that evening and was cleaning up the house. When I went to start on our bedroom, I found Goliath sprawled out on the bed. I told him to get down but he just raised up and looked at me. It seemed like all the frustration and worry he'd caused me surfaced at that moment. I was tired of playing games with him; tired of letting him manipulate me. It was hot, I was in a hurry, and I was angry. I went for his collar to pull him off the bed, and without warning he snapped at me. He bit my hand, but not seriously. It scared me to think he would actually do that. I realized then that he wasn't going to get any better. That's when I called you." Diana looked at me hopefully. "Is there any way you can get him leveled off again?"

It's not uncommon for my clients to ease up on their dog's discipline after they've had them home for a while. Most dogs can handle it pretty well without taking advantage of their added privileges. But in Goliath's case, it was a disaster. I needed time to find out just what it would take to straighten him out again.

"Why don't you leave Goliath here, then call me tomorrow morning. I'd like to see how much training he's retained, and also check him at feeding time before I give you a definite answer."

The next morning, Diana called exactly at nine. I was ready for her.

"Diana, I've never seen a dog regress as drastically as this one has," I said after she asked me what I'd found. "He even seems to be having memory lapses. I don't think he can be trusted anymore."

"B-but what should I do?"

"Well, as he is now, I would advise you to have him put to sleep."

Diana was horrified. "Put him to sleep?" she said with a catch in her voice. "Can't you do *anything* for him? It's *my* fault he went backward, not his." She was making a great effort not to cry.

I wasn't sure Goliath could handle another reprogramming. Yet deep down I felt it might be possible — *if* Diana would maintain the training once I succeeded. I had to impress upon her the importance of discipline in Goliath's case.

"I'll tell you what," I said. "I'll take him for training again. But I'm going to have to lay down some conditions for you to follow this time. The first one is that you do *not* give in to his demands anymore. I also want your husband and sons in on the training sessions. You're going to have to work together as a family to maintain his discipline. It's not going to be easy for him **or** me. He's nervous and unpredictable. But once I get him straightened out, it's up to you to keep him there. He'll never make it here a third time." I paused to let my words sink in. "Agreed?" I asked finally.

Diana let out a long sigh. "Agreed."

Goliath's retraining was a long and arduous process. It was not just a matter of teaching him the commands all over again; he already knew them. I had to break through the mental "fog" Goliath seemed to be in. I taught him the special "leave-it" command to keep him out of immediate or potential trouble. This was for motorcycles, bicycles, other dogs, and people. I worked Goliath mostly in the city where he was subject to all his previous temptations. I also trained him to stop eating any time I gave the "leave-it" command.

With his boundaries once again firmly established, and a solid master-dog relationship renewed, Goliath leveled off to the normal behavior he previously had. It took me longer to reprogram Goliath than it did to train him the first time. After he had left, I couldn't help wondering how he was getting along. Was Diana adhering to her part of the deal? My questions were answered several months later at Christmastime, when I received a card from Diana. She wrote:

Dear Bill,

You would not believe what a real pet Goliath has become. He still obeys all the commands you taught him. He really seems to want to please us. Thank you so much for helping us with his training. Merry Christmas . . .

For the next ten years, Diana sent me a card letting me know that Goliath was still obedient without one aggressive bone in his body, which her veterinarian was pleased with because one time Goliath had suddenly attacked and bitten him without being provoked.

DR. JEKYLL & MR. HYDE RAGE

An even more serious rage behavior can be caused by anger and fear due to harsh, dominant training methods. When you add pampering and catering, it can become a very explosive volcano. Such was the case with a Springer Spaniel named Doc whom I later renamed Jelly Bean. The following is excerpted from my book, *Jelly Bean Versus Dr. Jekyll & Mr. Hyde* which is a documentation of his once friendly behavior and his successful reprogramming. The following was written by his owner Richard A. Flinn:

"The sad part of Doc's career was a continuation of a series of increasingly negative and serious incidents. The older he grew, the more belligerently he reacted. Doc became more and more possessive and always needed to get something in exchange when we wanted to take something away from him.

"He had been living in a crate in the station wagon a large share of the time. Now, he did not like being confined in a kennel or crate. Although he would still jump over the tailgate into the crate on command, he would growl and bare his teeth as I locked the door. Every time I went up to his run to get him for training he would run back into his house and just roll one big, questioning eye at me. I would open the gate, move away, and *only then would he come*. I also remember one other bad reaction. He would tug unmercifully on his leash during our daily walks until I picked up a switch. Then he would cower and retreat so skillfully on the leash that I rarely could give him an authoritative whack.

"Now back to his behavior at a year-and-a-half. In addition to the growling upon kenneling, my wife Edwina had a shattering experience. She was in the back of our son's house (a confined space) with Doc, whose nylon collar had come off. As she tried to put his collar back on, Doc suddenly lunged at her and almost knocked her down. He pulled the sweater off her left shoulder and went for her throat. He would have seriously injured her if Jake, the neighbor's large house dog, which fortunately was in the same yard and close by, had not interfered and rescued her [Dog's Devotion & Spirituality Example], allowing her to reach the door and safety. She was very frightened and shaken up.

"When I heard Edwina's cries I rushed to the yard and took Doc out to the car. He looked bewildered and sorry and wanted to be friendly. I had him sit behind the tailgate. However, when I ordered him to jump into his crate he refused. I started to thump him. Suddenly he lunged at me, aiming at my throat and tearing my sweater. Somehow I got him in tow and attached an electronic collar which I had just bought. After getting him in his crate and locking the door he growled menacingly. That's when I shocked him for the first time.

However, the shock collar did not seem to have any curbing effect on his aggressiveness; it made it even worse. Doc continued to growl in his crate and showed no remorse.

"A few weeks later Edwina was removing ticks from Doc's body and experienced another assault. When she worked on his inner thigh to look for ticks, all of a sudden Doc changed personalities. His eyes narrowed and he jumped up on her, ready to bite. She was in a corner of the kitchen and alone, scared to death. She yelled 'hup' (sit) and stuck out her leg to keep him away from her body. She cried for help. Fortunately, I was in the next room and hearing her screams, immediately came to her rescue. The dog was still glaring at her when I snatched him and took him outside.

"The day after this event, Doc was again loving and sweet. We were at a loss to understand how this dog could change personalities so suddenly and frequently, from an obedient, faithful comrade and friend, into an unreliable, rebellious, dangerous adversary. We really became concerned that Doc might hurt us or others seriously, especially children. We could not trust him anymore. He had too often exhibited a split personality — a Dr. Jekyll and Mr. Hyde. We telephoned friends across the country for advice. The top veterinarian authorities, after hearing about the case, said there was no hope due to an apparent 'genetic failure.' Their recommendation was to destroy Doc."

Fortunately, Mr. Flinn did not accept these top drawer experts' advice and had me test and evaluate Doc. *The main two causes for the dog's Dr. Jekyll & Mr. Hyde behavior was that he was confused with mixed messages of humanization and being catered to.* Also, he was angry with his head full of rage at the painful/threatening training that he was forced to endure. By reprogramming Jelly Bean (Doc) through a series of corrective experiences based on mutual respect and trust, he was once again a friendly and loving pet. See photos, page 129.

CHAPTER 31(P)

EVALUATION OF AGGRESSIVE
AND VIOLENT BEHAVIOR

Aggressive behavior involves the use of force to coerce, control, or to kill another living thing. It is self-motivated and utilizes only the force necessary to achieve its goal, which is some type of material gain or sense of achievement. In the case of a dog, it barks excitedly when on the hunt or when chasing a cat up a tree. On the other hand, when it is cornered and threatened, it does not bark. Rather, it gives a warning growl and snarls, and will become violent if provoked beyond this point.

Aggressive behavior in humans is made more possible by depersonalizing the victim. For example, going hunting or fishing usually elicits no more remorse than climbing a hill to pick wild berries. On the other hand, the movie, *Bambi* personalized a mother doe, thus depicting her murder as a tragic act of violence. In acts of aggression, the object has a relatively impersonal identity, whereas with violence, the victim has a very real identity, if often a symbolic one, and is seen as having a source of power which was wrongly used to seduce, threaten or to harm the attacker who is now seeking vengeance.

Violence, by the definition given in this book, in contrast to aggression, is always motivated by defensive fear and rage. It most often results from a slow build-up of rage due to repeated provocation or to continual nursing of old hurts and wounds, accompanied by pleasurable fantasies of a particular act of violence against a specific target. In either case, there is a slow build-up of rage to a point where rational objectivity is lost and a sense of justification prevails over normal constraints. Finally, a level of tolerance breakdown occurs in which inner permission, accompanied by a sense of righteous conviction, allows the tightly coiled spring of emotional rage to release in a frenzy of unrestrained discharge which mimics closely the premeditated fantasy. In most cases, the violence is not lethal and consists only of a verbal discharge in which the tongue is used as a sword to cut deeply into the emotional belly of the perceived aggressor. This type of verbal violence is unfortunately common in the home environment, and can have devastating consequences upon children, whether or not they are the primary target. it creates deep emotional wounds which fester with fantasies of their own. Thus murder within one's own circle of family and acquaintances is still the major cause of homicide in this country, today.

To understand more simply how we all make the decision for or against violence almost daily, consider a situation in which you are repeatedly belittled by your boss in front of other workers. The process may begin within you with the thought, "One of these days, I'm going to let him have it back." This starts a mental counting system which accumulates tension as it records and magnifies each new hurt until your own personal tolerance breakdown point is reached and suddenly, for a seemingly minor harassment, you unleash your well-rehearsed verbal counter-attack upon your unsuspecting and startled boss. The threat of dire consequences will raise the tolerance breakdown threshold level, but sometimes this only postpones the inevitable, because at any tolerance breakdown level, by definition, the consequences have lost their meaning. This is why the perpetrators of violent crimes are often willing to sacrifice their own lives in the act of vengeance, or may make little initial attempt to cover up or to deny what they have done, so strong lingers the irate sense of self-justification. This is why punishment is not a significant deterrent to violence.

Violent behavior is always defensive behavior in the eyes of the perpetrator. It is seen as retaliation for a past or current insult, injustice, or humiliation. Anger is the natural biological and emotional response to fear, helplessness, humiliation or rejection. Rejection creates what psychiatrists call a "narcissistic injury." It can often result in violence or the threat of violence by ex-husbands and rejected lovers.

The fantasy of "teaching someone a well-deserved, painful lesson," can provide a temporary sense of satisfaction when no other avenues are open to express anger or to redress a wrong. However, every fantasy of violence, each time it is recreated in the mind, has an increasing likelihood of being acted out. When pushed to the tolerance breakdown point, the will is forced to make a critical decision of whether to act out in violent rage, or to crumble in tearful surrender, or to withdraw into deep depression. The decision depends upon the options open in terms of weapons and support and the direction in which previous fantasies have taken around this situation. Consent of the will in fantasy is consent of the will in action, given the right set of circumstances. Consequences are important only if they stop the initial train of fantasy. Violence can only be reduced when the education system teaches young children other options for expression and for coping with stress.

All behavior has a preceding history which gives clues to its motives, and a follow-up sequel, which either promotes or diminishes the likelihood of the behavior being repeated. Experience has shown that administering punishment during or after a given act may increase the apprehension or guilt experienced when repeating the behavior, but does not lessen its occurrence significantly.

The caveat must come before the behavior. There must be a prohibition at the point in which thinking about the behavior begins. To paraphrase the Bible: To sin in the mind is only a short step from sinning in the flesh. The only reliable deterrent to any behavior is to make it unthinkable. As an example, son- mother rape is unthinkable, and consequently, a rare event. There is rarely an act of violence that has not been fantasized and rehearsed in the mind, many times before its final execution. Non- violence must be taught to young children at every level. Acts of violence must be proscribed as unthinkable. Unfortunately, we have a television media which glorifies violence and which makes what was unthinkable in my generation, fashionable in the present one. I dread the day when daring writers begin challenging the taboo against mother rape.

The importance of making the distinction between violence and aggression is that each defines distinctly separate behaviors subject to different influences and motivations. Violence is motivated by fear, helplessness, and a sense of impotence. Its goal is punishment and revenge for a defeat, and never serves its perpetrator any useful, tangible gain. Violence is the last resort of failed aggression such as the burning of the oil wells in Kuwait, and the Nazi holocaust in World War II. The time when any leadership or regime must resort to violence to maintain its power base, its end is inevitable.

The outbreak of violence, which results from a tolerance breakdown within a particularly victimized segment of the population, is only a warning signal which will not spread further if properly addressed, instead of responded to with counter- violence. Punishment only inflames violence which, by definition, has already lost its rational fear of consequences.

Violence is best eliminated by prevention. This must begin with a stabilization of the family unit and followed by a renovation of our educational system, with a major focus upon non-technological communication skills. Opportunities for personal growth, for material gain, and for self-esteem through healthy aggressive channels must be taught and made generally available. Leadership training is important, also. Strong leadership may organize mass demonstrations, but with a control that keeps violence in check.

Violence once begun, quickly reaches an exhaustion phase, at which point it may be significantly diminished by concessions. But these concessions must lead to some form of meaningful empowerment. Again, grass roots leadership must be encouraged, not imprisoned. Leadership may result in aggression, but aggression is amenable to rules. The regime which is too inflexible to handle violence in this way will eventually crumble.

Aggression is the controlled use of power for personal gain. Aggression conforms to a consistent set of rules. Considerable aggression is tolerated, even admired, in our society so long as it remains disciplined from overstepping its boundaries into violence. Aggression by individuals, corporations, or organized crime may be altruistic, selfish, hedonistic or asocial, but is still influenced by the norms and regulations of the greater society. It may involve the constant testing of every rule, and a repeated attempt to expand existing boundaries and limits, but never directly attacks the system itself, with which it enjoys a parasitic relationship.

Aggression by the established bases of power in our society, which include our large corporations, has become increasingly self-serving, and relatively indifferent to the health of the planet or to the people left homeless by their bulldozer policies. Contrary to the political attitude over the past ten years, which has brought our country to the brink of moral and financial ruin, it is definitely the duty of government to protect the safety and the rights of its people by maintaining strong regulatory powers over every activity which affects the health, wealth, and the environment of the people. It requires strong and courageous political leadership to maintain the type of discipline and balance of all business enterprises which will ultimately serve the best interests of each of them.

The burden of responsibility rests upon our educational system, which must begin with the young in inculcating ethical and spiritual values, a sense of moral conscience, and the attitude of cooperation and service into the fabric of their self-concept. However, it is the schools which have failed our society in ignoring the real developmental needs of our children who pass through their critical stages of growth with a lack of self-discipline, a disrespect for authority, and a "me-first," attitude.

Aggressive behavior by large corporations, which results in the denuding of our rain forests, the contamination of our drinking water and the pollution of our atmosphere, is a far more serious problem than the violent behavior of victimized minority groups protesting against inequality. Once a disadvantaged group attains a strong leader and assumes an organized and planned direction toward empowerment, its behavior can be labeled as aggression. But, what's the fear? History has shown that the fears of the establishment are always unfounded. Killing the leader only delays the inevitable and increases the potential for violence.

Organized crime, like large corporations, has its own leadership, organization, rules, and discipline. Both live symbiotically within the system, and except for an occasional investigation and indictment, remain relatively untouched, so long as they refrain from violence which arouses public outcry, and also if they do not directly attack the system. They are both subject to the influence of legislation, legal rulings, public attitudes regarding their products, and the threat of specific penalties.

The most readily available legal mode of aggression open to the average citizen in our country is to engage an attorney. The attorney has replaced the hired gun. The more money you have, the bigger the gun you can afford.

CHART OF CHARACTERISTIC DIFFERENCES
Aggression vs. Violence

	__Aggression__	__Violence__
Personality Type:	Stable	Unstable
Motive:	Expression of Power	Perceived Injustice
Goal:	Personal Gain	Revenge
Emotion Before:	Excitement	Rage
Emotion After:	Exhilaration	Release of Tension
Brain Mechanism:	Attack	Defense
Ego State:	Controlled	Dyscontrol
Attitude to Target:	Indifference	Obsessed
Reaction to Consequences:	Concerned	Indifferent

AGGRESSION OR VIOLENCE

Q & A

Circle one:

A or V   1. The Gulf War.

A or V   2. Deer hunting.

A or V   3. Parent disciplining a child.

A or V   4. Man kills a jewelry clerk during an armed robbery. When asked why, he replies, "She didn't follow the rules." When asked whose rules, he replies, "My rules."

A or V   5. A homeless girl kills another homeless girl in order to take her sweater.

A or V   6. Dan White kills Mayor Moscone after the Mayor refuses to reinstate him on the Board of Supervisors.

A or V   7. Saddam Hussein's torching of the Kuwait oil wells.

A or V   8. Date rape.

A or V   9. A man in a wheelchair shoots his wife for threatening to leave him.

A or V   10. A young man returns to his high school to kill the history teacher, who flunked him.

A or V   11. A brilliant teenager kills himself after losing a debating competition.

A or V   12. A mother tells young children playing noisily to keep quiet. They ignore her. After the sixth warning, she rushes into their room and spanks them.

A or V   13. A wife, nagging her alcoholic husband in front of the children, to stop drinking.

A or V   14. A high school girl fatally stabs a friend who won the head cheerleader position, over her.

A or V   15. A "hit man" for organized crime interviewed on TV wearing a mask, says that he feels no guilt for killing.

A or V   16. The Los Angeles police beating of Rodney King.

ANSWERS:

1. AGGRESSION: It was purportedly the only rational decision left open to protect the rest of the world, and was controlled so that only military targets were hit. However, whether an excessive amount of force was used is still being debated. The importance of this question is that if answered in the affirmative, the action becomes an act of violence, and violence is deplored by the world community.

2. AGGRESSION: As a sport — without intent to cause unnecessary suffering, and provided rules and regulations are followed regarding season, weapons used, and number of kills allowed.

3. AGGRESSION: Discipline is an example of positive aggression. This is a two-way gain made possible by mutual respect. The same is true for competitive sports between players who respect each other.

4. AGRRESSION: Although not socially condoned, this was an unemotional act for personal gain, by rules which he announced beforehand. He "had a job to do," and no excessive force would be used if everyone "follows the rules." This callous attitude is a throwback to primitive dominant behavior.

5. AGRRESSION: An example of how "cold-blooded" aggression devalues life for personal gain. Empathy, respect, and value for life needs to be taught at an early age.

6. VIOLENCE: The motive was revenge upon a specifically selected target with no possible gain for anyone.

7. VIOLENCE: Revenge for a failed aggression with no perceivable benefit to anyone.

8. AGRRESSION: An example of the selfish seeking of pleasure, which is becoming increasingly more common in young adult males. There is callous disregard for the rights and feelings of the other person, but usually, there is no intent to cause suffering, and most likely an unawareness of the actual harm being done. It is the result of an undisciplined mind giving license to a normal instinctive drive upon a target of opportunity. In the past, women rarely complained because they believed that they would be held responsible because men are not expected to have any control over their sex drive.

9. VIOLENCE: An act of revenge for rejection. He justified his action when interviewed later, in jail, "She was killing me by what she was doing."

10. VIOLENCE: Senseless killing for no gain by an emotionally disturbed young man.

11. VIOLENCE: Anger turned against the self for not living up to performance expectations.

12. VIOLENCE: A common example of a parent who does not know how to properly discipline her children. Instead, she lets them push her to her tolerance breakdown point, which brings anger and a feeling of justifiable assault. Punishment is always the last resort of failed discipline. It has its place if unemotional and if the rules have been made clear beforehand.

13. VIOLENCE: Nagging is a form of belittlement and degradation which serves no useful purpose other than a release of pent-up anger. She feels like a victim, helpless and trapped, and wants her

husband to at least suffer some guilt. The core problem here, is that the wife is being forced to assume the dominant position, which she resents. Similarly, a wife will nag a weak husband in an attempt to make him a man. She feels disillusioned and betrayed by being shackled with a little boy instead of a supportive adult.

14. VIOLENCE: The Performance Trap has taken on such an emotional charge that, even at the high school level, success or failure is a matter of life or death.

15. AGRRESSION: Like a hired mercenary, he was paid to do a job.

16. AGRRESSION: According to the jury, policemen are licensed to use force, including guns and billy clubs, to protect themselves and the public. They are not licensed to use excessive force. The tape appeared to indicate that they did use excessive force. And so the debate goes on.

CHAPTER 32(M)

CANINE PSYCHOANALYSIS

One of the most frequent questions asked of me is, "How do you psychoanalyze a dog? They can't talk." True, they can't talk in the same way that humans communicate by voice. A dog cannot relate his dreams, frustrations, fears, and angers — the process established by Sigmund Freud, the father of human psychoanalysis. Yet, similar to human behavior, dogs use a mode of non-verbal communication which, by the way, is 55 percent of our own way of expressing what we may be feeling but not verbalizing it.

According to Dr. Albert Mehrabian, noted researcher in non-verbal communications at UCLA, our body language always expresses the truth. We all understand the non-verbal shaking of a fist or the blowing of a kiss or the outstretched arms of a welcoming hug. I remember especially one thing that my co-author and spiritual friend, Ernie Pecci, M.D., said at one of the process sessions in 1971. "Your body (language) always communicates and expresses its hidden feelings, revealing to the trained eye the exact truth of the person's thoughts and emotions. Although I have only a little knowledge of metaphysics, I do know that 'thoughts are things' and that most action is preceded by thought, either consciously or subconsciously."

With this additional understanding, I observed Ernie's body movements while he was instructing the group which was seated in a large circle. I noticed that before he finished talking with an individual his left foot would already be turned and angled to the next person who was sitting to the left.

After witnessing the same pattern four consecutive times (which, to me, constitutes an established pattern) I mentioned my observation to a friend sitting next to me. While I was describing it, Ernie turned around and gave me a very direct stare and then turned back around to finish his conversation. I had just witnessed his psychic/sense awareness which is a sense perception tuning into another form of communication beyond the five senses. On a higher degree, dogs operate in the same way.

Thus, in psychoanalyzing problem dogs, sensing the inner being of a dog becomes part of the broad picture of psychological testing/ evaluation/consultation with both dog and client.

BEGINNING

It usually begins with a telephone conversation with the potential client. I strive to gain insight into the client's set of values regarding dog ownership and see whether they have a "know it all" attitude or instead, a willingness/openness to my concepts and philosophies.

Because most dog behavior is an effect, the cause of which can be found in the environment of which the owner should be in charge, at this point I will advise some callers that I cannot be of service to them and suggest they may be able to sort out their dog's behavior by reading my book *Jelly Bean versus Dr. Jekyll & Mr. Hyde.*

The reason I do this is because through my experience with closed-minded dog owners, I have found the axiom, "**PEOPLE CHANGED AGAINST THEIR WILL ARE OF THE SAME OPINION STILL**" to be a truism. The other thing I am aware of is the saying, "a positive person seeks a way to solve the problem. A negative person finds an excuse or an alibi as to why (s)he cannot do something."

SECOND PHASE

While the potential client is still on the phone, I explain the importance of case histories of the dog's behavior — the problems that have taken place, the type of reprimands given, and the training background of the dog.

All co-owners of the dog, such as husband, wife, and responsible children are required to write his/her individual history of their pet. The importance of this is that I sometimes find a dual standard behavioral requirement which can cause confusion for the dog. Also, because dogs form different relationships/rapport with each family member, there can be totally different images of the dog's behavior.

If all owners consent to write a case history, my perception of their willingness, open mind, and their ability to make a dual commitment is reinforced. At this point I consider that I can usefully be of service to them and an appointment is made.

ARRIVAL

My evaluation of the dog's behavior begins the moment the owner opens up the car door. I first take note of the following:

a) Does the owner just open the door and let the dog jump out without any leash to restrain it?

b) Does the owner snap on the leash in order to control the dog's movements?

c) I watch for the dog's position on the lead in relationship to his owner. Is he out front and pulling the owner to the bushes alongside the parking lot? or,

d) Does the dog look to the owner as to which way to go? or,

e) Is the dog so fearful it's afraid to move? Next, I start evaluating the dog's sense of territory.

TESTING

TERRITORIAL: Does the dog mark all the trees and bushes before entering the building? Does it mark the inside of the run as well as the outside? Does it challenge other dogs farther away than 5 or 6 feet? Does it act as though the whole kennel is his and everyone else (dogs and people) is trespassing? If so, this dog is highly territorial and it will be necessary to shrink its territory within acceptable limits.

When the owner walks the dog through the kennel doorway, I watch for two responses.

DISCRIMINATION: It is natural for a dog to be discriminating when approaching new people and surroundings. Thirty seconds should be enough time for the dog to size up the situation. The longer it takes, the more cautious and/or suspicious the dog. On the other hand, some dogs do not bother to discriminate and will plunge into a situation or greet a person with complete abandon. This is again evaluated when I put the dog into a run.

FEAR: The other thing I watch for is fear: does the dog tuck its tail between its legs; does the tail drop down or does the body (language) get more upright and the tail stiffen up, ready to take on anything that is on the other side of the door, showing no fear, but only an aggressiveness? Now some dogs will have been in situations such as visiting a strange home or a visit to the veterinarian, and because of their fear, will bolt through the door in order to get past the closeness of the door jamb. These two mini-tests are repeated two more times as I lead the dog through two other doors before putting him in his run.

The time for testing varies according to the dogs behavioral problems, from a minimum of 4 hours to several days of on and off testing in order to be certain that reprogramming would work. However, extended testing/evaluation cases are very rare and are for dogs that express a combination of vicious intent toward humans, especially a member of the immediate family.

I do not permit the owners to observe the testing mainly because of the dog's ability to sense them even if they are hidden in my office or sitting in the parking lot. After the dog has been in his own run for a while, I return to him and take him out for some more defined tests. Some dogs start acting up as soon as their owners depart — howling and/or barking — which permits me to evaluate the emotional relationship between owner and dog. I have found after testing several thousand dogs that there are two groups with several shades of grey between them:

A. EMOTIONAL DEPENDENCY: This characteristic generally becomes apparent after the owner has departed. The dog will begin to whine or howl while alone in its run. I note how long the mournful wails last. To find out if the emotional dependency has been conditioned by the owners, I take the dog into the training area, kneel down and talk to it in a high, gushy voice while stroking it. An emotionally conditioned dog might respond by groveling, urinating, or whining excitedly.

B. EMOTIONAL DEMAND: This is also caused by emotional conditioning, but is characterized by a slightly different response. Whereas the emotionally dependent dog vocalizes its complaint randomly and mournfully, the emotionally demanding dog has a definite purpose. It will bark awhile, then look around to see if anyone is coming to rescue it.

Because each dog is different and there are different behavioral problems to varying degrees, and taking into account the age of the dog, some of the following tests may be skipped altogether according to how well the dog responds to my earlier handling and his willingness to cooperate. I am able to add a test or two later in the day whereas in the morning tests, because of the hazard of being bitten, I will skip any test that may trigger the dog's fear and/or viciousness.

The length of testing time also varies with the average being 10-15 minutes of testing and then giving the dog an equal time to relax. This time-out also helps me to evaluate the dog's ability to recall what was taught 15 minutes earlier. This is re-evaluated each testing session — looking for an increase in memory retention. The results are combined with the main memory retention test.

MEMORY RETENTION: I walk the dog in heel position for about 5 minutes, then purposely weave in and out around some posts. As I continue, I suddenly side-step so the dog is caught on the other side of the post. I do *NOT* jerk it back into the heel position; the dog is led back. After a rest of 10-15 minutes the dog is taken out again. Does it lead me out to the training area? Does it recall the entrance door? Does it still get caught in the posts, or does it remember to side-step them with me?

WILLINGNESS TO SERVE/WORK: As I walk the dog in the training area, I notice its overall attitude. Is it watching me constantly? Does it look eager, alert?

By contrast, a dog unwilling to work might lag, look browbeaten, and be generally uncooperative. One that pulls and is easily distracted is involved in its own self-interests (scents, sights, sounds).

WILL TO POWER (W.T.P.): As I take the dog out of the run into the training ring, does he pull me around, leading me especially to the door leading outside? When he does pull out front, I will stop walking, which in turn stops him and then I do an about-turn and begin to walk in the opposite direction. A high will to power dog will again run out in front of me and take his pulling/leader position. Then after 5-8 feet I will stop and reverse my direction. The number of about-turns I take before the dog figures it out will indicate its intelligence to a limited degree. Another way I test the W.T.P. is to walk the dog around the training ring and then stop and face him. If he knows the command 'sit' I put him in a sit/stay command and then I make the following test:

TEST OF WILL-TO-POWER: I take hold of the muzzle gently but firmly with the thumb over the top and the fingers underneath. I slowly move the head in an up and down motion, then side to side. A dog that allows me to do this with little or no resistance has a low will-to-power. The more resistance the dog exhibits, the stronger the will. *I do not use this test on overly aggressive dogs.*

ATTENTION SPAN: I have the dog sit and I face him in a kneeling position, then gently grasp the muzzle and look steadily into his eyes. I note how long the dog returns the gaze before looking away or fidgeting. A dog must be able to focus its attention on the trainer a minimum of 3-4 seconds in order to be able to learn. Also, I note eye expressions. Some will express fear, others, a dislike of my holding the muzzle.

Some dog owners are surprised by how short their dog's attention span was even though the dog had been obedience trained and had been titled C.D.X. (Companion Dog Excellence in A.K.C. trials). I do not do a hands-on testing of either the attention span or W.T.P. if there is any indication that the dog's fear and/or aggression would be triggered.

SENSITIVITY TEST: In most cases this is tested the second or third time the dog is taken out. As I am walking the dog, I casually (but suddenly) do an abrupt left turn and bump the dog. How does the dog respond, and to what degree? If there is no reaction, I do some heeling for a few minutes and then bump again. The less of a response, the more insensitive the dog, and vice versa. Again, if the dog is overtly aggressive or fearful I will skip this test.

TOLERANCE: This test is mainly for growling or biting dogs. It is done along with the sensitivity testing. What I am looking for is his capacity to absorb the sudden bumps I do in the sensitivity testing. Another way I test the dog's tolerance is to check his ability to be trained in a 4 to 5 minute period. This is the minimum time that is needed for conditioning the dog's mind and to instill new behavior, especially if the past history is of an aggressive, vicious nature. If the dog will not tolerate being trained for this length of time, I consider the dog not reprogrammable. He could never be trusted not to bite again. Such was a 7-year-old Great Pyrenees dog that after four brief workouts lasting a few minutes, refused to heel for even one minute. There was a possibility of something being physically wrong with him. Yet, as far as his testing went, he expressed a tolerance breakdown long before new behavior could have been instilled in his mind.

FEAR TESTS: When the dog first enters the kennel and goes through the various doorways for the first time, I already have some input as to his fear response level. I add to this data after walking the dog for approximately 10 minutes on leash. I will stop with the dog standing alongside of me. Then I will gently touch his shoulder. If the dog is fearful, his adrenals will be surging, causing a muscle reflex or twitching. Should there be no response I will again walk him for a minute or two and stop. This time I will lightly tap/touch his upper rib cage — looking for a twitch/muscle reaction. I will repeat this test, going lower and lower until the response/reflex level is determined. A shoulder area response would indicate his biting was a survival reaction versus a low adrenal response (hind quarters) of an act/intent of will to power (W.T.P.). With a Dr. Jekyll and Mr. Hyde, or highly aggressive/vicious dogs, I *do not* test the adrenal/fear level.

Again, one is surprised at the number of highly trained and obedience-titled dogs that are still adrenalized and are fearful of unknown noises and sudden touch in testing.

TEMPERAMENTAL TEST: This characteristic will become apparent while performing the other tests. How well does the dog tolerate my bumping into him? I give several light jerks on the leash as I walk it. Does he balk and refuse to heel? Does he sulk and lag behind? How long does it take for the dog to come out of its mood? Was I able to encourage him to come back into heel position? If the dog takes 3-5 minutes to recover, he is very temperamental. Should the case history reveal that the force/dominant, heavy jerking and choking were the methods used in his training, I will forego this test.

Willingness to serve (W.T.S.) work is constantly evaluated during each session. It's the dog's overall attitude. Is he watching me constantly for directions/commands? Does he look eager, alert? How many about-turns when testing his W.T.P. does it take for him to stop taking the lead and pulling me? Is the dog constantly involved with its own self interests such as sniffing every post, looking around at the different objects I have in the center of the testing/training ring? What's his attitude when I approach the kennel run to take him out and work with him? The second time, sixth time, tenth time, does the dog show an increased tolerance of my handling him or, does he express increased dislike of my taking him out and working him?

Each time I take the dog out for 10-15 minutes, I am looking for changes where the negative behavior lessens and the positive behavior— such as W.T.S., attention span and memory retention increases. At the end of the day these variables give me a good composite of the dog's psychological/emotional personality which I then compare to the dog's case histories. Like a yardstick divided into three equal parts, the third part is consulting with the owners as to their beliefs/desires/expectations. I explain the three basic reasons for almost every behavioral problem in dogs that I have worked with:

1. LACK OF TRAINING: Permitting the dog to teach himself. Expecting him to sort out the daily events and responding with the right behavior. To know when he did something wrong and to correct his own behavior. Many dog owners have informed me that they base this 'training' on what they read in dog books; *i.e.*, xyz breed is highly intelligent with a good temperament and makes a good pet for children. The fact is, a highly intelligent dog does not automatically operate with good manners — just the opposite is usually true. The more intelligence an untrained dog has, the more likely he is to run the human family due to his instinctual pecking order needs.

2. *IMPROPER TRAINING:* Especially the abusive alpha wolf/dog training methods that for some reason many dog behaviorists/trainers and owners have adopted in the past 20 years (see Alpha dominant training).

3. *HUMANIZATION:* This is a very common practice today, when the dog is an emotional/human substitute, perhaps for a single person who does not have a relationship with the opposite sex. In almost all cases a woman will own a male dog. A man will own a female dog. What takes place here is the polarity balance of the animal kingdom, plus and minus (+/-), male being the plus, female being the minus which does not mean negative or opposite energy. In regard to the physical, I had only one case where a form of sex had taken place. Catering, pampering and coddling is the cause of most behavioral problems. Dr. Pecci calls it buying love with human beings/child substituting. This type of treatment, in most cases, is indulged in by couples as contrasted with a single person who has a direct need of emotional human companionship.

In almost all of the dogs I have tested, I have determined that the cause of the problem behavior was a combination of lack of training combined with humanization and 65 - 70% being used as child substitution were either small or toy breeds. Humanized dogs are so worshipped by their owners that even the thought of a collar around their loving pet's neck and forcing him to walk on a leash is unbearable and out of the question. Improper training using the alpha wolf/dominant methods, coupled with humanization, were the causes of problem behavior for most medium and large size dogs.

DENIAL

This is the toughest part of consulting with dog owners/trainers who suddenly have a Dr. Jekyll & Mr. Hyde on their hands. It seems that some people are so used to *fixing the blame* rather than taking the responsibility to *fix* the problem, that when I explain the basic three reasons for problems, they still try to fault the dog. I believe the reason for this denial is the refusal to accept the fact that they would have to make personal changes within themselves in order to correct their dog's behavior.

This is why I often recommend Dr. Pecci for personal psychotherapy for owners with "crazy" dogs. The reason for denial is usually based on the fact that dog owners are often unable to comprehend or accept the tremendous power they have in influencing their dog's behavior.

The first thing I explain is the importance of their own attitude and emotions in setting the tone for the relationship. If we accept the basic premise that all healthy dogs have an innate desire to please their owner, whey then do we fault the dog for undesirable behavior!

CHAPTER 33(M)

DISCIPLINED MIND

Conditioning the disciplined mind is not a form of punishing the animal, but putting the dog through a series of *corrective* experiences based on mutual respect and trust. This form of training creates a behavioral control of the dog to first discriminate, and assimilate before it responds to anything new. This is diametrically opposite to an untrained or improperly trained dog that reacts mainly from the survival instinct of self-preservation. I look at the mind like a muscle that when not exercised will atrophy. By training a dog on a repetitious schedule daily, 7 days a week, each session builds on the previous one to where the mind is disciplined to be strong and can control its old behavioral response and replace it with a new one.

The most important thing I watch for when training or reprogramming a dog that has previous behavioral problems is *I do not* get involved or reinforce any of the old behavioral responses including snapping, biting or growling. If I did, this would only keep the old behavior alive, which with the trigger stimulus the dog would express its negative behavior. All training sessions are done in a non-threatening, peaceful and serene environment. This, of course, requires that I remain balanced, peaceful and have a self-disciplined mind to control any of my negative behavioral responses which could very easily trigger an old pattern of aggressive or fearful behavior in the dog.

To give a clearer picture of how the disciplined mind is formed, I liken it to how a candle maker dips a length of string, which becomes a wick, into a vat of hot wax which is controlled at a certain temperature. As soon as the candle is withdrawn, it is allowed to cool, after which it is again dipped, then removed. This process causes a very thin layer of wax to adhere each time. After a number of dippings the candle now has the thickness that is desired.

This methodology of building layer upon layer is how I condition a disciplined mind based on mutual respect and trust. The most beautiful reward after such conditioning is the way the dog relates to all other beings with the same behavior of respect and trust. Some dogs will never revert even when tempted (see Servitude Trap).

This type of training controls the adrenals which, when triggered, causes the dog to react based on the survival instinct.

CHAPTER 34(M)

BEYOND THE PECKING ORDER

The innate will-to-serve mankind, as the most important genetic behavior trait of the dog to man, can not only control the will-to-power, but also other natural instincts, and can even be developed to be stronger than other inherited traits. By conditioning the will-to-serve, the dog becomes able to control such genetic behavior patterns as his chasing instinct and inbred fighting instinct.

Chindo is a living example of how genetic behavior patterns can not only be overridden but can even be changed through learning, thanks to the uniqueness of the will-to-serve.

Major Jack Craft became aware of and interested in the Chindo breed shortly after his arrival in Korea in 1969. The Chindo is the national dog of Korea, originating in the little island of Chindo off the southwest coast. These dogs are noted for their loyalty, adaptability, cunning, and intelligence, paired with fighting spirit, hunting ability and a reputation as ratters.

The major got his genuine Chindo as a seven-week-old male puppy. This puppy was completely different from any other puppy he and his family had ever owned. For example, he was already housebroken by his Chindo mother. From the beginning he maintained a rigid set of behavior standards for himself, which the major had never before observed in a dog. The puppy would not eat stale food or table scraps and ate only at night. No other animal was tolerated near his food. He accepted human intrusion, however. The most unusual thing about this pup was that no other dog could dominate him. He never gave in, or begged, or ran. He was very independent and quite aggressive with the other dogs and animals in the neighborhood.

Chindo grew into a beautiful dog of 50 pounds. He loved to hunt, especially rats, but hated loud noises and car rides. When he was kept on a leash or in the house, Chindo was submissive, a warm and friendly dog. He never gave more than a warning growl or bark at a stranger because he respected man. He had a different attitude toward animals, however, demonstrating that the animal world belonged to him.

When he was an eight-month-old puppy, he was threatened by a full-grown hunting dog. He immediately had the hound on his back, slashing him open before holding him by his throat. One day the major lost his temper with Chindo and grabbed him by the flank, a spot about which the dog had always been very protective. Chindo snapped at him. The major did not want a biter as a family dog, but a dog he could walk comfortably — one that would obey him and not try to attack or challenge other animals. Therefore, he arranged for his psychological reprogramming.

Training Chindo was a new experience for me, because he was so different from any other dog that I had ever encountered. Chindo was not a "macho" dog with something to prove. For Chindo, fighting was a way of life — as natural as wagging his tail.

To prevent Chindo's fighting instinct from being triggered by facing living objects, he was kept in a specially designed run with a panelled front gate and sides to block the view of other dogs and the deer that lived and grazed in our fields.

In the beginning of his training program my first step was to slowly develop communication with him through basic obedience. This was later complemented by some special commands. I then succeeded in walking him around the ranch animals without having him show any interest in them. One time I was walking Chindo in our field looking for a sitting jack rabbit. My intention was to startle the rabbit and when he began to run, to give Chindo his special command "leave it." Chindo was heeling properly, but all of a sudden, like a lighting bolt, he advanced and seized a gopher snake, gave it one snap, shook it, and tossed it out of our way. Then within the same moment he fell back into the heel position. All this happened so fast that I stood there for a couple of minutes before I could fully understand what had taken place. I had never before, or since, experienced a dog moving with such speed.

238

A harder, more time-consuming task, was to persuade Chindo to leave dogs alone, because of his inherited instinct to challenge any dog that encroached on "his" territory. Therefore, it was extremely difficult for him to understand that it was wrong to attack other dogs. It was very hard on him too, considering the conflict between his desire to please me and his natural impulse to fight.

Fortunately, his will to please was so high that he was able to overcome his genetic and conditioned instinct to fight four-legged animals. It was a painstakingly slow process (three months of therapy training) until Chindo had finally learned not to react to aggressive, challenging dogs. A crucial point in this whole procedure was that Chindo was never physically punished for his fighting tendency.

The major and his family were very pleased with their "new" Chindo. One day he called me and proudly related an incident that had just taken place. He had put Chindo on a down-stay command in his back yard when his attention was diverted by a visiting neighbor. Some time had passed in conversation when all at once the major remembered he had left Chindo in the most vulnerable position for a dog, especially a fighting dog, just in time to witness a German Shepherd giving Chindo the sniff test. Chindo merely glanced at the dog and laid his head on his paws. The major gave Chindo the "be good" command (to be on the safe side) before chasing the German Shepherd away. He then praised Chindo lavishly. Perhaps that was Chindo's greatest victory.

Next, an adopted female beagle was accepted by Chindo as part of the family. They even played together. A Siamese cat was another happy addition to the household. Chindo lived in friendship and peace with these animals and remained an amazing, beautiful, living proof that it is possible to transform a merciless fighter into a gentle friend and protector.

SUMMARY

1. The will-to-serve can be used to overrule genetic behavior as shown by the case of Chindo.

2. It was natural for Chindo to fight and kill because he was bred for this purpose.

3. When his owner attempted to punish Chindo, triggering his survival instinct, it was natural for him to bite in self-defense.

4. Instead of using force and punishment in his reprogramming, which would have compounded Chindo's problem, his willingness to please was properly developed. It then could control his will-to-power and strongly inbred fighting instinct.

CHANGING DOG BEHAVIOR PROBLEMS
WITH RESPECT AND TRUST
(Lisa Scherer's story)

It all started five years ago with my first dog Sable and my first obedience class. Sable is an American Pitbull Terrior mix whom I acquired through a friend. I decided to join a local training class and teach her the basic obedience commands.

With my second dog Hawk, an Australian Shepherd, I became interested in competing in obedience trials. As my interest grew I kept looking for better ways to train my dogs. I attended more classes locally, and in other areas. I read books and attended seminars. The methods I was taught always seemed harsh to me, but being a novice I did what I was told. I kept looking for a better way of training, one in which I worked with my dogs in a way they understood, not against them.

I had also begun to do rescue work through my local animal shelter for the American Pitbull Terrier and the American Staffordshire Terrier. I had rescued a four-month-old male "pitbull" who I named Samson. Samson is a wonderful dog with a great personality except for one drawback; he had a problem controlling his excitement. When I first brought him home, he was so hyper I could not control him. He would fly from room to room in my house destroying everything in his path. His favorite thing to do was to get a running start and fly through the air and land on my husband who was sitting on the couch. I tried everything I knew to stop this behavior: collar corrections, verbal corrections, scruff shakes and even attaching a leash to him so while he was in mid-air he would hit the end of the leash and be brought to an abrupt halt. None of these things worked. In fact, he would just keep coming back for more, faster and harder. I was at my wits end; I didn't know what else to do.

Then I read the book, *Jelly Bean versus Dr. Jekyll and Mr. Hyde* written by C.W. Meisterfeld. Mr. Meisterfeld is a dog psychoanalyst located in northern California. He has been analyzing and rehabilitating dogs for the past 35 years. The light bulb went on. Here was the training philosophy I had been looking for. It made so much sense. I finally found a method that worked with dog behavior that wasn't dominant or harsh in any way. After finishing the book, I called Mr. Meisterfeld. The next thing I knew, Samson and I were enrolled in his upcoming Canine Workshop.

Once I was in the workshop, my living conditions with Samson at home had to change. C.W. had us remove him from living in the house and asked me to place him in a kennel of his own. This way he wouldn't have a chance to perform any of his old tricks. Then we were put on a strict daily working schedule, where I trained Samson using methods based on mutual respect and trust. At the same time I was training him, I was strengthening the good behavior and attitude I wanted, while gaining his respect.

As Samson's life was changing, so was mine. There were changes that I had to go through to properly train Samson. I had to become non-judgmental and not respond to his actions with anger or corrections which I was so conditioned to do. I had to teach myself patience and realize that changing his behavior would take time. I had to learn to evaluate any problems I saw in the dog and find the cause of why he was behaving in this way. You see, there is not a "quick fix" to changing a dog's behavior problems. You have to find the cause and get rid of it, and then put all of your energy and focus into strengthening the good behavior that you want. With time, the good behavior will become strong enough and the behavior problems will start to go away. The cause of Samson's behavior problems was me. I had treated him like a baby and spoiled him rotten. Therefore, he felt that he was in charge of my house and the rules. He didn't respect me or my position as leader of the household.

This changing process took a while for both of us. Once my attitude changed, so did his. Dogs use sense perception to read you and your moods. Before, when I was getting angry at Samson for destroying my house, he would sense this anger and become more rebellious. Once I quit using anger and force and I approached training him with a different attitude, he became more receptive to my teachings. He started to enjoy our sessions and looked forward to pleasing me. Fortunately, Samson has a high level of servitude and this was starting to show. With the dominant training I was doing before, I was actually reducing this high servitude and increasing his will to power and rebelliousness. We had gotten to the point where we were just battling wills. But now things were changing.

Samson started to calm down and listen to me. He then got to the point where he would catch himself getting out of control and correct it without any verbal reminder from me. As each of these transformations took place, I was more and more convinced that this is the correct way to train dogs. The time and effort in training that I had been putting in was beginning to pay off. Here was this puppy who had previously been hyperactive and uncontrollable becoming this happy, well-behaved young dog.

As time went on, he started treating my other dogs with respect. There were never any challenges made or power struggles to be had. If another dog challenges him dominantly, he will just turn away. He is not interested in returning the challenge or fighting them at all. Instead, he will just go on his way as if they were not even there.

The first time I saw this behavior of walking away, I was proud of him. I also knew that this was the dog training philosophy I was looking for.

Samson has always had an intense fetish for tennis balls. If you have one in your hand he will follow you anywhere. If he has one in his mouth he will not drop it unless told to do so. We take long walks around the vineyards near our house and he even carried his ball with

242

him on one of those. When he had to pant he just held the ball between his front teeth and still kept going.

Every so often I will let Samson and Pogo (an American Staffordshire Terrier I have) out to chase the ball together. This is something they both enjoy. Even with Samson's intense love for the tennis ball, if Pogo gets to it first Samson will turn away. He does not try to steal it or cause a fight.

He now can be let in the house without going out of control, and he listens to my commands without an ounce of rebelliousness or defiance.

Samson's display of respect towards humans and other animals is the way it should be. He gets along with all of my dogs, cats and other various farm animals. I also trust in him one hundred percent that he would never aggressively harm a person. This is the behavior that domestic dogs were meant to have. One which is based on servitude and respect. Samson has turned out to be a wonderful dog who is a joy to live with.

Since graduating from the workshop I have used these methods on other "pitbulls" I have rescued with great success. One of these cases was Bubba. Bubba was a one-and-a-half-year-old male "pitbull" who was abandoned by his owner and left tied to a tree for two weeks before coming into the animal shelter. When I saw Bubba for the first time he was very shy and full of fear, but I saw a special dog underneath all of that. I knew he would make someone a great pet. The day I went to rescue him, he was afraid of getting into the car. When I got him home he would not walk with me through our garage with the doors opened on each end. He didn't trust me, or anyone for that matter.

I worked with Bubba daily using the same methods I had on Samson. The first time I put a chain collar and leash on him, he tried to run away. When he came to the end of the leash and the collar tightened up he screamed as if I was hurting him. I took my time training Bubba. We took each step very slowly. First heel, then stand and stay, then sit and so on, all using respect and trust. Not once did I ever jerk his collar or correct him for anything. Over time, his trust in me grew and his behavior blossomed. He was changing into a totally new dog. He now looked forward to our sessions together and he was very happy the whole time he was working. We eventually got to the point where he would go into the garage with me without showing any fear. Then it got to the point where I had to teach him to "wait" while I opened the door. Otherwise, he would burst through the opening into the garage and bounce around happily.

One day while we were practicing our lessons, I noticed that he was distracted by my truck which was parked in the driveway. Whenever he would heel, he would turn to look at it. I walked him over to the truck and when we got there he was very happy and kept looking back and forth from the truck to me. I opened the camper and the tailgate, and to my surprise, he jumped right in. Then he looked at me as if to say, "Well, aren't we going to go somewhere?" I couldn't say no, so I took him for a drive up and down the street. From that moment on, Bubba loved going for rides in the truck. It was as if his fear had just disappeared.

Between the time since I had taken him from the shelter and the time of this incident, he had not been in a car at all. I did not try to force him to get over his fear of cars. As his trust in me and his own self-confidence grew, all due to patience and consistent respectful training, his fear of vehicles just went away.

Another instance of Bubba's growing trust was at my in-laws swimming pool. One day while we were swimming, he jumped into the water and sank all the way to the bottom of the pool. When he came up and I helped him out, he was terrified. He wouldn't even come close to the edge. I would take him with me when I went swimming after that, but I never forced him into the water. Then one day while I was sitting on the pool steps relaxing, he came up to me and put a paw on each shoulder. This was his sign that he wanted me to take him in the water. I picked him up (which was not easy), and we went into the pool together. I held him as if he were a baby. There wasn't any fear at all. In fact he like it. From then on, if I was sitting on the steps, he wouldn't leave me alone. Slowly his fear of the water went away and with time he went into the pool on his own.

It took me five months to rehabilitate Bubba and get rid of his fear so I could place him in a new home. During these five months, Bubba received consistent obedience training using only Meisterfeld's philosophies. I never tried to force him into a situation where he was fearful, and I never tried to "socialize" him. If I had done these things without having the proper respect and trust first, I would have increased his fears and never made progress. By using these philosophies of Mr. Meisterfeld's in the proper way, he learned to trust. As his trust grew, his fear went away on its own. I never focused on his fears, I focused on the good dog that I knew was underneath all of the fear and that is what he became.

I found a wonderful woman who fell in love with him. I worked with her and instructed her on the proper way to train him. When Bubba went to his new owner there wasn't any fear left. He trusted everyone. You could take him anywhere; the veterinarian, the groomers, other peoples houses, and he was always happy and friendly. I have kept in touch with Bubba's new owner and the trust that he had for me has transferred over to her. He is today still the same happy, obedient dog that he was when he left me to go to his new home.

I have also rehabilitated other "pitbulls" I have rescued with the same result. Using Mr. Meisterfeld's philosophies, I have been able to make these dogs into the great pets that they were meant to be. For the first time in some of their lives they've learn to be able to trust humans, because I never gave them a reason not to.

With all of the dogs that I have trained using these methods, none of the dogs are aggressive or dominant towards other dogs or people. By using mutual respect and trust, not dominance, to train these dogs, I did not reinforce that dominant aggressive behavior. I reinforced their respect for me and other people, as well as other animals.

I am still an active rescuer for the American Pitbull Terrier and the American Staffordshire Terrier, and in promoting the good nature and temperament of these wonderful breeds. I am now also teaching obedience classes using Meisterfeld's philosophies. In my course, I teach the students how to have the proper relationship with their dogs based on respect and trust. It is nice to be able to teach them that they do not have to dominate their dogs to have control over them. They do not have to become the so-called "pack leader," they need to become the dog's master.

Mr. Meisterfeld's philosophies of dog training are a must for every dog owner to know. I highly recommend the book *Jelly Bean versus Dr. Jekyll & Mr. Hyde* (Subtitled, "Written for the Safety of our Children and the Welfare of our Dogs") to anyone who is involved with dogs, from the pet owner to the dog breeder. In this book you will find the keys to opening the door on really understanding dog behavior. It will also lead you down the right path for your future in training and living with dogs. Meisterfeld's way of training is the correct, humane way. It makes so much sense. Through respect, trust and kindness you can achieve so much more than from dominance and forcefulness. No matter what kind of breed or problem, the results are always the same: a happy, obedient, trustworthy animal.

CHAPTER 35(M)

DOG'S DEVOTION AND SPIRITUALITY

Ever since man and dog have been recorded in history, the dog has been working with and serving mankind in some capacity. On the walls of Egyptian tombs are paintings of dogs showing their servitude for man. There are scenes depicting dogs hunting, herding, and protecting their human families. Today, dogs have been developed to further work and serve man in these and more specialized capacities.

As far as breed specific behaviors goes, an amazing example is the Komondor. Man has taken a great deal of time and patience to selectively breed a dog who cannot only herd and protect his charges, but also has the appearance of the livestock he protects. The Komondor has a very long, thick, white coat which covers him from nose to toes, thus making him blend with the livestock. His sheep-like exterior actually makes him a "dog in sheep's clothing," and hides him from the would-be sheep predators. What I find most remarkable about this breed is that he will live with and protect his flocks for weeks and even months without the presence of his master.

Not only does the Komondor watch over the flock, he provides for himself by hunting on his own. His food consists of small wild game and rodents. When water is in short supply or unavailable, he is accepted by the ewes who will allow him to nurse from them. It's apparent to me by this point that this dog and the flocks he protects have a wonderful working relationship. This unique breed of dog is now employed for his high servitude by livestock breeders and ranchers all over the world.

Man's best friend today still serves in the roles portrayed on Egyptian tombs. Our dogs today hunt, retrieve game, round up cattle for milking and sheep for sheering, guide the blind, assist the deaf, and perform many varieties of other services for man.

A dog's servitude toward man is not just breed specific, such as the herding and guarding of the Komondor. Almost all of the dogs used to serve the deaf as hearing ear dogs are taken from animal shelters and have completely unidentifiable lineages. Therefore, what makes these dogs unique is not their breed specific abilities. What makes these dogs unique is the fact that they are willing to serve man in a working, master-dog relationship regardless of breed characteristics. This evidence is enough for me to believe and know that no matter what the breed, a dog is a dog, and any dog can learn a task and serve man willingly.

Beyond the dog's natural servitude for man lies an even higher altruism. There are many stories which, no doubt, we have all heard throughout the years that indicate that our dogs can be more than just service animals. To me, these stories show that our dogs operate on a higher plane at times, an intuition which shows itself through the dog's altruistic deeds for which it was not taught. It's almost like a spiritual parent watching over us, especially our children. The dogs seem guided intuitively by this spirit to protect and save human lives.

Ken-L Ration, a branch of the Quaker Oats Company, has been recognizing and honoring this type of dog altruism since 1954. Each year a committee reviews many incidents of dogs serving beyond the call of duty. The following cases have been taken, with permission, from Ken-L Ration/Kibbles 'n Bits Dog Heroes. I have added my interpretations and comments to each case:

TANG

Winner of the first annual Ken-L Ration gold medal award as America's Dog Hero of the Year was Tang, a huge, friendly collie from Denison, Texas. Owned by Air Force Capt. and Mrs. Maurice Dyer, this dog, possessing a protective instinct to a remarkable degree, saved no fewer than five children from death or severe injury.

Four times he leapt in front of swift-moving automobiles and thrust his powerful bulk against a child to push the tot to the curb just split seconds before tragedy could strike. On another occasion, he planted himself squarely in front of a parked milk delivery truck and refused to budge, barking loudly all the while. When the puzzled driver alighted to ascertain the cause of the strange behavior of the normally friendly dog, he found that a two-year-old girl had clambered into the back of his truck, from which she would almost certainly have fallen. The moment she was removed, Tang ceased his barking and returned placidly to the sidewalk.

Tang's story is a heart-warming one. The Dyers had lost their own collie, and, in their grief, could not bring themselves to adopt another. But a veterinarian finally persuaded them to "just look" at Tang, who, little more than a puppy, had been the victim of mistreatment and was completely mistrustful of humans, especially children. "Something in his eyes" reminded the Dyers of their own lost dog, however, and with numerous misgivings, they took him home.

Affection and kindly care worked wonders on Tang, and in six months he had developed into a powerful but friendly dog, who without any training whatsoever, had established himself as the protector of children at the air base in Alaska at which Capt. Dyer was stationed. As speeding army trucks rumbled past the homes of the military personnel, Tang would herd his charges back from the road, and twice he actually pushed tiny tots from directly in front of the automobiles.

Transferred to Perrin Air Force Base, Capt. Dyer took up residence in nearby Denison, Texas. There, the Dyers and their neighbors were witnesses to the sight of Tang saving two more children in similar fashion.

Self-appointed nursemaid and baby-sitter for the whole neighborhood, Tang became a real celebrity in Denison. And when the news came that he had been unanimously selected as the winner of the first national award for dog heroes, the children of the neighborhood organized an impromptu parade for him.

This great-hearted dog passed away in 1958, but the children he loved did not forget him. He was laid to rest in a peaceful glen, and around his grave the children play to this day. Tang would have wished it no other way.

Author's Comments: Although Tang used his natural herding abilities to bring the children back into their proper surroundings, how did he sense their danger from moving vehicles? And, how did he

TANG — 1954

know to stall the parked milk truck? And what makes a dog place himself in the way of danger without putting his own survival instincts first?

TOP

A courageous, child-loving Great Dane named Top, from Los Angeles, California, who saved two children from death or severe injury by two heroic deeds within eight weeks, was the winner of the Ken-L Ration gold medal in 1969.

Owned by a young German immigrant actor, Axel Patzwaldt, 25, the harlequin-type dog will always limp noticeably on his right rear leg, which was shattered when he was struck by a truck as he pushed a young girl from the path of a swift-moving vehicle. But the injury failed to prevent Top from initiating the rescue of a two-year-old child from drowning just eight weeks later.

The huge dog's exploits began on an April day when an 11-year-old neighbor girl was allowed to take him for a walk. A short distance from home, she started across the street, not noticing that a large truck was swiftly approaching. Suddenly realizing that the child was unaware of her danger, Top barked loudly, jumped in front of her, and pushed her backwards out of the way. She was unhurt, but Top was not so lucky - the truck hit him, breaking his right rear leg.

He was rushed to an animal hospital, where the leg was set and placed in a cast. His master took him home, and for seven weeks Top limped about painfully. Then, one week after the cast was removed, Patzwaldt let him out into the apartment house backyard, which contained a swimming pool. Just a few seconds later, Top came bounding back to the door, soaking wet and barking at the top of his lungs.

Patzwaldt and other residents ran to find out the reason for his noisemaking. They followed the excited and wildly-barking dog to the pool, and looked down to see the apparently lifeless body of two-year-old Christopher Conley, of the same address, lying on the bottom of the pool in six feet of water. Obviously, Top had leapt into the pool

TOP — 1969

in an attempt to aid the tot, and failing in that, had summoned help by his loud and continuous barking.

A former lifeguard, Patzwaldt dove into the pool and brought the child out. Although the boy was apparently dead, the man began mouth-to-mouth resuscitation efforts while others called a fire rescue squad. By the time the firemen had arrived, Patzwaldt had managed to arouse a spark of life in the tot. Rushed to Citizens Emergency Hospital in West Hollywood, the child began to show signs of improvement, and eight hours later was pronounced out of danger.

The first Great Dane ever to gain this honor, the young dog later was forced to undergo an operation necessitated by an infection that developed from broken ribs sustained in the auto accident. But though he still wore the stitches when he appeared at the dinner in his honor, he strode majestically to the platform and stood quietly in a statuesque pose as the gold medal was placed about his neck.

When asked why Top was given his unusual name, his proud owner explained that a friend had given him the choice of an entire litter and that he had selected Top because he was "the top of the whole group." Subsequent events have vindicated his judgment.

Author's Comments: What enabled Top to realize that the neighbor girl was in danger when she was unaware of her impending doom? Even though Top was severely injured by a truck when saving the 11-year-old girl, he placed himself in another potentially life-threatening situation only eight weeks later. Why? How did this Great Dane know that the 2-year-old was in danger when he found him in the swimming pool? Surely Top had seen people who were not in danger swimming in the very same pool. And, as our Dane fancier readers will know, Great Danes are not generally known for their water sports abilities.

BUDWEISER

A John's Island, S.C., Saint Bernard named "Budweiser," that pulled a 4-year-old girl from a blazing house *and then returned to similarly rescue a second child,* today was named one of five finalists

BUDWEISER — 1973

in competition for the 20th annual America's Dog Hero Award in 1973.

Budweiser gained hero status when an explosion sent flames shooting through the home of Mr. and Mrs. B.M. Carter, owners of the 14-month-old dog. At the time, six of the Carter's grandchildren were in the house with Mrs. Carter. Budweiser charged into the house, grabbed the youngest child, Linda Lawson, by her shirt and pulled her out of the burning home to the safety of a neighbor's yard. He then raced back into the blazing house and pulled 5-year-old Joyce Hinson by the arm out of the house and across the yard. In the meantime, Mrs. Carter rounded up the other four children and herded them to safety.

When Budweiser tried to enter the house a third time to rescue the family's Chihuahua, he was driven back by intense flames. Within 30 minutes the roof collapsed and the house was a total loss.

Author's Comments: Saint Bernards have long been known for their rescue abilities, and this is still not so unusual. What is unusual in Budweiser's story is the fact that he entered the building two times to save two small children, but tried in vain to enter the house a third time to save the family Chihuahua. What made this giant dog run through the fire he would so normally and instinctively avoid? And, what kind of bond made him want to save even the other family dog?

WOODIE

Woodie, a collie mix owned by Rae Anne Knitter of Cleveland, was named the Ken-L Ration Dog Hero of 1980. The canine was honored for the courage and devotion she displayed when she leapt off an 80-foot cliff to rescue Rae Anne's fiance, Ray Thomas, from drowning.

One afternoon, Rae Anne, Ray and Woodie were out walking along the nature trails in the Cleveland Metroparks Rocky River Reservation. Ray, an amateur photographer, wanted to capture the spectacular view from atop a steep shale cliff; Rae Anne waited on the path with Woodie while Ray positioned himself for the shot.

WOODIE — 1980

Ray disappeared over the top of the hill. Suddenly, Woodie began twisting and tugging to escape from Rae Anne. The persistence of the usually well-behaved dog convinced Rae Anne that something was wrong. She let go of Woodie and followed her over the top of the hill.

When she reached the brink she looked in horror at Ray lying face down and unconscious in a stream 80 feet below. By his side was Woodie. Ray had lost his footing and plunged over the side, and Woodie had taken the jump herself, sensing her friend's need.

Woodie had broken both hips in the fall, but struggled to nudge Ray's face to keep it out of the water. She then began to bark frantically, calling for help. When the rescuers and Rae Anne reached the injured pair, they agreed that Woodie's instinctive concern for Ray had saved the young man from drowning in the river.

Ray spent two months in the hospital, undergoing treatment for multiple fractures in his back and arm. Woodie, who suffered internal injuries and broken bones, has undergone a personality change, as well.

"She's more affectionate than ever," Rae Anne says. "It's as if she realizes how lucky she is to be alive."

Author's Comments: How did Woodie know Ray was in danger and injured even before she arrived by his side? Furthermore, how did Woodie know to keep Ray's face above the water level to keep him from drowning? What made Woodie almost sacrifice her own life in order to save that of a human? Whatever the answers, this experience brought a new meaning of life to both Ray and Woodie.

REONA

A two and a half year-old Rottweiler named Reona showed her intelligence and bravery during the devastating earthquake in California, October, 1989. This special dog from Watsonville, California, was selected from over 100 entries following an annual search by the makers of Ken-L Ration dog foods for the most heroic dog in the nation.

Reona is credited with saving the life of 5-year-old Vivian Cooper. Hearing screams from across the street after the earth's first

REONA — 1989

jolt, Reona bolted out the door, jumped three fences (something she had never done before) and bounded into Vivian's home.

The terrified child was standing in the kitchen when 102-pound Reona pushed her against the cabinets and sat on her. Seconds later, a large microwave oven on top of the refrigerator came crashing down where Vivian had been standing.

Reona, a true hero, saved Vivian's life in more than one way. Vivian suffers from epileptic seizures that are often triggered by excitement. According to the child's mother, a seizure could have been fatal since she could not reach her, and Vivian's medications were scattered everywhere. Fortunately, Reona had arrived on the scene and was able to calm the frightened youngster. Although Vivian had been afraid of Reona in the past, she hugged the dog tightly and buried her head into Reona's fur.

Reona's heroic act has left a lasting impression upon little Vivian. "Now there's a bond between them that just won't quit," said Jim Patton, Reona's proud owner.

According to the Pattons, Reona has come a long way since they adopted her just over two years ago. She was an abused puppy, and it was one week before they could even touch her.

Author's Comments: Even though Reona must have heard more than one person's screams, she ran to the aid of Vivian, a five-year-old. Why? Reona had to jump across three fences to get to Vivian and rescue her. What's even more remarkable, Vivian was calmed by the presence of Reona of whom she had previously been afraid. What made Reona choose Vivian among all the helpless persons in the earthquake, and why do they now have a bond that cannot be broken? Chance? Coincidence? I don't believe so.

SHEBA

Sheba, an Alaskan Malamute from Nashville, Illinois, knocked down 20-month-old Cassandra Vance and covered her with his body to protect her from a swarm of yellow jackets. Sheba received 27 stings and nearly died, but Cassandra received just one! Sheba was a runner-up for 1991.

Author's Comments: How did Sheba know that little Cassandra was in danger from the yellow jackets? And even if he did know the danger, how did he know to cover the child with his own body? What made Sheba keep the child covered while all the while he was being stung by the yellow jackets? Why?

In each story, the dog went far beyond a normal servitude, even to the point of putting its own life in danger. Why? These dogs have nothing to gain by helping another living being, in fact they could have lost their own lives. What led these dogs to serve us in this most special way? I cannot find a logical reason for these deeds, no matter how much I search. These dog deeds are nothing short of the dog's way of being an altruist — doing for others and expecting nothing at all in return. Surely, the dog is man's best friend, and one of God's gifts to the human race.

CHAPTER 36(P)

BEYOND THE PECKING ORDER

What is a human being, and how do we differ from the animal kingdom? We can say that we have highly specialized brains with large frontal lobes and extra convolutions in our gray matter which enables us to engage in abstract thinking and complex reasoning. Perhaps our dilemma is accurately symbolized by the Great Sphinx of Egypt: a spiritual being entrapped in an animal body.

In any event, until we understand more about the nature of our animal body and its built-in patterns of coping and survival, we will continue to be deluded by the notion that our behavior is largely determined by free will.

We are gifted with a mind that can control every facet of our physical body. Yet, without a respectful awareness of the innate instincts and drives of the physical body, and without proper training and a disciplined mind, sooner or later it is the emotional needs, the drive for power, the sexual urge and the survival instincts of the physical body that will ultimately run the mind.

Humans normally have a strong intellectual defensive mechanism which serves to hold in check instinctive impulses and drives so that they can behave in a socially acceptable manner. The result, for the average person, is inner conflict and neurosis. Why are animals, who apparently have no such defenses, less troubled and able to behave more humanely to one another in social structures, than do humans? Perhaps it is because animals do not experience an alienation between their inner world and their outer world of nature. And, why don't animals, like most humans, have to expend immense psychic energy in suppressing an inner volcano of rage that threatens constantly to erupt to every provocation? Perhaps, if humans within a given family or social system accepted each other unconditionally as animals accept one another within their social groupings, there would be little need for the defensive functions of the ego and for the constant storing of rage.

Until we accept the inseparable relationship of the physical body to nature, and obey the laws governing all of nature, we cannot prevent its breakdown and its aging prematurely despite all of the technological advances of medicine.

As each civilization becomes more complex, it paradoxically becomes more dehumanizing, more stressful, and more out of touch with the natural order or things. It eventually begins to decay from the center outward, as its core breeds malaise, depression, and violence. This is the problem facing all of our major cities today: the insidious corruption of human values breeding self-alienation and violence. None of this is natural to nature. Rather, it is the result of severing our bond to nature and to the natural flow of the underlying order which sustains life on this planet.

The mind of man has the power to create beautiful edifices, spacious cities, and complex social systems. But, lest he be constantly aware of the danger, he too easily becomes entrapped in these structures of his own making. His identity becomes lost in the artificial fabric of a great, creative cultural illusion which now veils him from his true identity and his primordial interdependence with nature. We live in a materialistic world dominated by the left brain. From a very early age children are taught to exercise their left brains for spelling, math, and the memorization of endless mimeographed information at the exclusion of their right brains. Yet, it is our right brain, the creative and intuitive aspect of our nature, which is by far our greatest asset and the source of every major new discovery. A balance between the two is needed. And the proper use of this balance, under a disciplined mind, yields the greatest fulfillment of our potential. young children are primarily right-brained, which means that they experience the totality and wholeness of nature without dissecting it. Once they make the shift to the reasoning intellect, they cease to experience the real world, except in terms of what they tell themselves.

One of the problems with our educational system today, is that it puts data into the left brain as answers, instead of questions. This not only limits, but obstructs, the creative function of the right brain. It is not so much what schools teach as what they do not teach that makes a tragic waste of the precious opportunity they have to influence positively, the minds of young children during their most receptive and impressionable formative years. Schools might better serve society if they focus upon the real lessons which children need to learn:

1. They need to learn to appreciate their growing bodies and to respect their individual differences of color, size, shape, talents, proclivities, and sensitivities.

2. They need to understand their emotions and feelings, learn to articulate their needs and fears, and to trust their inner knowing.

3. They need to learn how to ask the right questions instead of being fed answers and labels that take away all the awe and the mystery of the life around them.

4. They need to look inward as well as outward, and to explore all the levels at which communication can take place.

5. They need to know their connection to nature, their bond to one another, the grandeur of their being, and the value of their caring.

6. They need to know of their innocence, of the fallibility of adults, and of what is them and what is not them.

7. They must dare to have dreams, to honor the desires of the heart, and to learn the meaning of love at every level.

8. They need to learn about kindness, sharing, responsibility, and self-discipline as the foundation for maturity and success as adults in the world.

Perhaps, if there were one word to describe what is needed most in the world today and which is lacking at the level of the family, among the various subgroups in our society, and among the nations of the world, that word would be "communication." Paradoxically, the explosive growth in the technological transmission of information around the world has nearly made close interpersonal communication obsolete.

During the first five years of schooling, children should spend more time learning to communicate with each other than listening to the teacher. Interpersonal communication is the basis for learning. During the first two years of school, all of the major modes of communication are stifled to the exclusion of technological communication.

My own report cards were always down-graded because of "conduct." I was always "caught whispering," which was treated like a mortal sin. I wanted to discuss, share, get involved. I must have heard the teacher say, "Mind your own business, Ernest," ten times a day. In retrospect, I was trying to mind my own business. Everyone I can see, touch, or reach with my whisper is my business, part of my world, a brother or sister sharing the life experience. We are trained to go through life in our own little booths, trying to mind our own business. It makes us paranoid. People who live in an apartment house in a city of a million people are lonely because of this. A woman is being knifed on the sidewalk in New York with 35 people watching from their windows, every one of them minding their own business until she is dead.

Why is everyone so busy? Where are all the people rushing to go? They are afraid if they stop that they will get in touch with their loneliness. We don't have time to really make contact, to really touch each other, or to fully savor life. Certainly, we are not taught this in school. Life is outside the windows of the dreary rectangular classroom. Finally, the bell rings announcing the end to one more long day of confinement.

Those whose parents want to push them toward success, will have precious little time to savor the outdoors because of the added burden of homework. What if a child could be made to study endless hours until he read the entire Encyclopedia Britannica? What then? Very few highly successful men would credit their high school or college classes for their success. In any event, six hours per day of linear thinking is sufficient for any child.

As the unit of the family goes, so goes the social structure. Children search for a sense of significance in the eyes of the adults about them, as they reach out for emotional bonding and love. When they see eyes clouded with fear, worry, and indifference, their spark of innocence becomes encapsulated in a protective wall. Something in them begins to die as anger covers their hurt feelings.

Civilization, with its social constraints and enforced, suppressive learning environments, promotes the progressive dehumanization of children. There is a loss of bonding to nature, and with this, a loss of essential being and worth. They become out of touch with inner reality at the cost of serving an outer reality. Spiritual values are reduced to empty concepts and religious ritual. They develop a negative emotional state which, like heavy smog, clouds their consciousness with fear, confusion, overwhelm, and apprehension. Behind it all is the heart's aching for spiritual nurturance. Street drugs and prescription drugs are used in large quantities to calm the mind's frantic clamoring for the harmony which only nature knows. In every human being there is inner loneliness and an inner desperate search for something, anything to fill the void left by the loss of essential purpose and being. Once the tie to nature is severed, the resonance with the inner and the outer world is lost, and with it, an instinctual sense of one's ground of being. The outer world is seen as an enemy, a competitor, a barrier to the fulfilling of one's inner needs. To attack or to blame someone out there becomes the way of easing a conflict within. The stresses of day-to-day coping creates inner conflict, irritability, frustration, and a desire to give up or to resort to violence. It is as if something imprisoned inside is crying out for expression regardless of the consequences. Creating more prisons is not the answer.

Psychiatrists are only recently placing emphasis upon the exploration of the human qualities of basic goodness and love. And the power of love when activated can overcome the forces of hate. Researchers now seriously term love as a nutrient and compare its role with Iodine and Vitamin C. There is some evidence that love even influences the growth of children's bones. It certainly affects a child's ability to learn in school; it is the foundation of emotional health, the magic wand that lifts the curse of self-dislike.

Perhaps it is important that we learn to get in touch with our own potential for anger, perhaps to avoid hurting others, perhaps to recognize the violent potential of those we work with every day, perhaps to be aware of our own triggers that can result in brief lapses of rational thinking, perhaps to have compassion for the actions of those who feel less lovable than ourselves.

Anger is not something we must deal with in order to proceed along the business of human social interaction, but rather, the disease itself, the causes and cure of which deserve our prime attention and focus.

Albert Camus, in his play, *The Plague,* states it well:

> ... each of us has the plague within him; no one, no one on earth is free from it. And I know, too, that we must keep endless watch on ourselves lest in a careless moment we breathe in somebody's face and fasten the infection on him. What's natural is the microbe. All the rest — health, integrity, purity (if you like) is a product of the human will, of a vigilance that must never falter. The good man, the man who infects hardly anyone is the man who has the fewest lapses of attention. And it needs tremendous will power, a never-ending tension of the mind, to avoid such lapses.

That is why it is so important that we learn to understand the capacity we all have to love and the power inherent in loving to dissolve anger and fear.

We are human beings in an animal body, and as such are subject to all of the baser emotions common to the animal kingdom. But whereas anger and fear are survival mechanisms to provoke attack or to assist in flight in lower animals, these emotions serve no useful purpose in man. We are unique from all other species in possessing a center of higher awareness, intuition, knowing, and will. Then, too, we have an intellect that weighs, judges, and is capable of rational decisions. Only when we lose sight of the special nature of our being, do we regress into helplessness and fear and then bring senseless suffering to ourselves and to others. The motives of the animals are based upon survival of the species and the pain/pleasure principle. In humans, the prime purpose of all activity is toward freedom to restore to oneself the full awareness of who we are. The pain/pleasure principle only temporarily satisfies the pain, despair, and loneliness created by our deeper memory of our separation from whence we came and the yearning for the oneness we once knew. So, sense pleasures, physical pleasures are sought as a desperate measure to temporarily try to satisfy something that can not be satisfied in this way. The yearning, the emptiness, the longing, the loneliness, the incompleteness, the dissatisfaction is still there behind it all.

Konrad Lorenz, who pointed out the universal existence of an aggressive instinct in the animal kingdom, later acknowledged that ". . . greater feelings of love and friendship for others may prove incompatible with the expression of overt aggression." Ideally, as we evolve as a people, the extreme polarities, such as master-slave, gradually merge into a brotherhood of equality. And this is the inner battle we all must resolve, the struggle between self-serving isolation or cohesive communion with one another.

In the course of an average lifetime each person plays many roles in a variety of relationships with others, including parent-child, husband-wife, teacher-student, and boss-employee. These relationships are held together by our gregarious nature and an innate need to create and to sustain a meaningful social bond. Through these experiences we learn something about giving and receiving, the rewards of service, the responsibilities of authority, and the right use of power. Rollo May stated, ". . . no human being can exist for long without some sense of his own significance." As humans, we must learn the true meaning of power. The misuse of power leads to estrangement and an endless search for significance through control, domination, and violence. The right use of power is for empowerment. One's own sense of significance can be best measured by the willingness and the desire to enhance the significance of others. In the animal kingdom, power is expressed through instinct and emotion. In the spiritual man, power is expressed through reason and love.

However, fear and competition closes the heart. With the heart closed, man becomes enamored with himself. Then the greater the wisdom, the greater the pride. When the heart is open, the greater the wisdom, the greater the appreciation and the awe of the fathomless mystery of life all around us.

Integrative Therapy Presentations/Seminars

Over the past 25 years, Dr. Pecci has evolved a system of studying consciousness by examining its imprinting upon and within the physical body. His system of evaluating the aggressive, creative, intellectual, and emotional energies through an examination of body structure and energy flow has been called "Holographic Body Mapping," in Michael Talbot's recent book, *The Holographic Universe.*

During this time, he made regular appearances on KGO's "Owen Spahn" talk show and was the first psychiatrist dealing with emotional problems of listeners in a talk show format. During the 1970's he was a much sought-after speaker for leading New Age conferences, including "Mandala," in San Diego, "Cypress," in Carmel, The Association for Research and Enlightenment, in Arizona, and the "Continuum of Consciousness" series conducted by John F. Kennedy University. Dr. Pecci self-published numerous manuscripts and booklets distributed at his lectures. Two of his self-published books, *I Love You/I Hate You* and *Meditative Insights*, have already sold six thousand copies each, and the requests remain brisk.

Out of his wide range of clinical experience, coupled with his knowledge of metaphysical principles, Dr. Pecci has created an intensive training by which the average person can understand and break free from the chains of childhood programming in a period of 12 weeks. He calls this "The Integrative Therapy Process," a transformative tool, so powerful and effective, that it has been called, "The next step in psychotherapy."

Dr. Pecci conducts one and two day workshops in a variety of settings involving peer relationships and employer and employee relationships, including major corporation and educational schools and colleges.

For additional information write/phone/Fax:

Integrative Therapy Seminars
2910 Camino Diablo, Suite 100
Walnut Creek, CA 94596
Phone: (510) 935-8781
Fax: (510) 935-7408

Complete Comprehensive Two Day Workshop

. . . a unique investment in the future of "MAN'S BEST FRIEND"

CANINE BEHAVIORAL PSYCHOLOGY
- Fascinating facts about the canine mind
- How to fulfill your dog's psychological needs
- How to test and evaluate canine behavior
- Causes and cures of canine mental stress
- Human/canine interactions that cause behavior problems

PSYCHOLOGICAL DOG TRAINING
- The basic principles of psychological dog training
- How to apply techniques of psychological dog training
- Special commands for specific behavior problems
- How to apply the Pavlov principle for positive results
- How to rehabilitate shy, fearful, aggressive dogs and more

VIDEO PRESENTATION OF PROBLEM DOGS
- Hyperactivity and Rage Syndrome
- Dr. Jekyll & Mr. Hyde Behavior (JELLYBEAN)
    - Before and after Reprogramming
- Brain-damage (misdiagnosed)
    - Before and after Reprogramming

PSYCHOLOGICAL TESTING/EVALUATION/CONSULTATION
(dogs to be selected from attendees)
- Aggressive Dog
- Fearful Dog
- Hyperactive Dog

For additional information write/phone/Fax:

M R K PUBLISHING
448 Seavey
PETaluma, CA 94952
(707) 763-0056
FAX: (707) 763-1539

270

Home Training Program Package

AUDIO CASSETTE ALBUMS

Album #1   Canine Behavioral Psychology   (4 Cassettes)
Album #2   Psychological Dog Training   (4 Cassettes)
(Recorded live at the California State University in Sacramento)

VHS VIDEO CANINE CAPERS

"Sir Walter" (costume dog) helps trainer demonstrate in a humorous way how improper obedience training causes behavioral problems. Using the Pavlov principle the dog's willingness to be leash-trained is being reconditioned. Sir Walter and his trainer demonstrate, also, how even a shy retriever can be reprogrammed.

This video comes with NON-COMMERCIAL PUBLIC PERFOR-MANCE PERMISSION.

BOOKS

Psychological Dog Training   Behavior Conditioning with Respect & Trust (by C.W. Meisterfeld)

Tails of a Dog Psychoanalyst   (by C.W. Meisterfeld)
This collection of 38 true case histories deals with serious and humorous incidents with dogs which are entertaining and educating at the same time.

As a Man Thinketh (by James Allen)

Price per package including two day UPS shipment: $295.00
(CA add tax)

To prevent shipment delay due to check clearance, please send Money Order or Bankdraft (prices subject to change).

MEISTERFELD & ASSOCIATES
448 Seavey, Suite 9
PETaluma, CA 94952
Tel. (707) 763-0056
FAX (707) 763-1539

BOOKS

- For one copy of *Crazy Dogs & Crazy People* — $26.95 (please add $4.50 for shipping).

- For 4 copies sent to the same address, we pay the shipping.

- For larger order/discounts, please contact the Publisher (below).

Other books by C.W. Meisterfeld

- *Tails of a Dog Psychoalalyst*
  Hardcover — $19.95. ISBN 0-901292-2-7

- *Jelly Bean Versus Dr. Jekyll & Mr. Hyde: Written for the Safety of our Chidren and the Welfare of our Dogs*
  Hardcover — $19.95. ISBN 0-9601292-5-1

- *Psychological Dog Training: Behavior Conditioning with Respect and Trust.* — $18.00. ISBN 0-9601292-6-X

(California residents, please add sales tax)

Please add for shipping:
    One book — $4.50
    Two books — $6.00
    Three books — $7.00

M R K PUBLISHING
448 Seavey
PETaluma, CA 94952
(707) 763-0056
FAX: (707) 763-1539